making peace with paradise

an autobiography of a california girl

tania runyan

ts T. S. Poetry Press • New York

T. S. Poetry Press
New York

Tspoetry.com

© 2022 by Tania Runyan
All rights reserved.

Cover photo & design: L.L. Barkat / llbarkat.com

ISBN 978-1-943120-62-8

Runyan, Tania
    [Nonfiction. Autobiography. Culture.]
    Making Peace with Paradise: An Autobiography of a
       California Girl / Tania Runyan
    ISBN 978-1-943120-62-8

to my sister heidi, who gets it

I grew up five miles from the Pacific Ocean, hedged in by backyard bougainvillea, roses, and kumquats. My mother kept yellow African daisies in flower beds surrounded by the cool, succulent hearts of dichondra. Jacaranda trees dropped purple flowers, which, during our rare rain showers, floated like amethysts in the gutters. I wore sandals on Christmas.

But I dreamed of everywhere else.

In fourth grade, I saved up twenty dollars to buy the large red *Hammond Ambassador World Atlas* I spotted at Waldenbooks in the Westminster Mall. As soon as I brought it home, I lay by my bedroom's screen door that opened to our tropical backyard and started to explore. Soon I realized it wasn't the far-flung countries I was drawn to, but other states. States very different from mine.

The California two-page spread unnerved me. An inset diagram at the upper-right corner indicated the state's place on the globe: a gash of red against the curving green land, an open wound on the earth.

My imagination took refuge in places like Iowa, Nebraska, and Kansas. Kansas sat like a preschool rectangle, most of its counties similarly shaped and contained by perfect corners and lines.

I wanted to lie on the quiet blanket of Kansas with its quilted edges of farm towns and soda-fountain main streets, where families didn't yell or rip telephones from walls.

Of course, I didn't know about tornadoes or thunderstorms or slaughtering pigs in barns and frozen pipes. I just knew these places were clean and predictable and far. Towns like Plains. Crystal Springs. Hope. Towns where I could hide.

I didn't realize my home had a history of providing abundant food and gold to the world or that Hollywood was any big deal. I didn't know people spent their life savings to move here or that TV shows like *Three's Company* were cool precisely because they were set just miles from my house.

In middle school, I started collecting pen pals from all over the country. I also corresponded with a few kids from Paris and Tokyo. Mostly? I was interested in girls named Jane from the Midwest.

Tell me about fall, I would write. *Tell me about snow.*

Why? You live by Disneyland! San Diego! Mountains! The Beach!

But I often felt nervous passing through the hallway of my own home, and the Golden State was simply where I lived. For me, there was no California Dreaming. I just *was,* at the center of it all.

EARTHQUAKES

It felt like one of our big Afghan dogs had bumped into the couch, but the dogs remained snoozing in the grass outside, and the crystal pendants of the chandelier, which hung on the other side of the living room, clinked like tines on a plate.

I froze, *Ramona the Brave* in hand.

Had a spirit entered the house? My mother collected antiques, many of which haunted me in the small Orange County ranch. Trembling, I glanced at the Viking faces that jutted out from the mahogany arms of the brown velvet couch. The stern faces of ceramic Pekingese dogs on the brick mantel. The faces of hand-painted cats on decorative plates that spotted the walls.

She had accumulated most of these items years before I was born, even years before my sister's birth fourteen years prior to mine. My mother and her treasures had their own relationship. The chair she bought from an estate sale while she attended art school. ("I went without food for that one.") The tiny French perfume bottles she dug out of a dumpster, cleaned, and displayed in the bathroom, a glass menagerie filled with ancient amber liquids. It would be years before I'd realize that one of dozens of figures in the small curio cabinets in the entryway, a small black figure jutting from an alligator's mouth, was a slave in the process of being devoured.

For at least ten minutes after the jolt I sat, afraid to move, straining to hear the fading echoes of the big brass pendulum of the grandfather clock. Finally, my mother pulled into the driveway, home from her job at the interior decorating store.

"Mom, what was that?" I asked when she walked in, red hair bobbing. The front door jingled with vintage bells and tassels tied to the brass handle, and I folded my arms as she passed.

"It was weird, Mom. It felt like someone hit the house."

"Probably a little earthquake. I didn't feel anything in the car."

"The earth *moved*?" I twisted the end of my braid. "Why?"

She started to get Polish sausage, my dad's favorite meal, out of the fridge, moving about the kitchen briskly, her hair skimming the antique ladles and flour sifters that dangled from the ceiling. Soon my dad would come home demanding dinner. At two hundred and ten pounds, and over six feet tall, he downright knocked stuff off the walls.

"It has to let out the pressure."

"Why does the earth have pressure?"

"It's the way the land's formed, something like that," she said. "Don't stew about it."

And that was where we left it.

The pressure on the earth had been released through a right-lateral strike-slip fault some one hundred miles away near the town of Anza. A small, 4.8 quake, it was unlikely many other people in my town felt it. But alone in the house, I had shaken alongside the breaking earth, 1920s carnival glass looking on.

Sure, summer latchkeyism had its perks. Other kids had to play dodgeball in day camp. I spent the days eating as many popsicles as I could, watching Wheel of Fortune, writing plays, and reading. In the weeks following the quake, though, I padded across the marble and parquet floors, afraid I would somehow trigger another lurch.

"You're home alone because you're more mature than the other kids," my mom would say, and I'd let those words roll through my mind. Being smart and mature was a burden I carried with both pride and shame. In second grade, my teacher had kept me in during lunch to tutor other students. I loved and dreaded it at the same time. Tall, quiet and studious, I tried to pass myself off as older, and the teacher had been complicit in the ruse.

But suddenly, at age 9, I felt the need to hold up the house. I wasn't ready.

~

October 1. Sophomore year in high school. My friend Adina and I stood at her locker as she grabbed books for morning classes. Like all southern California campuses, Los Alamitos High is outdoors, classrooms opening to walkways and courtyards lined with lily of the Nile, lockers distributed in dozens of blue metallic pods over a number of acres. We wore T-shirts and sundresses as morning light poured gold across the campus. Adina took a last look in her locker mirror, pushing back a few black curls and blotting lip gloss. Then? The ground took a dip like a fishing boat or roller coaster, and my stomach seemed to bounce off the concrete.

"What? Who's jumping?" I yelled, furious with what must have been a football player's antics. But when I saw students scattering into the courtyard, some spinning and cheering "earthquake!" I clung to Adina's arm.

For the next ten minutes, the campus exploded with chatter. Kids in zero period choir said they thought the risers were getting pulled out from beneath them and rampaged toward the door. Kids in the parking lot said the asphalt turned to waves.

I stood outside biology class, afraid to enter. Was this a foreshock of what was to come? I had heard of the Big One, but it seemed far, too far to matter in my life. Now the familiar classroom became a potential deathtrap of concrete and exploding gas valves. When an aftershock hit right after the first-period bell, kids dove under the lab tables with delighted screams, then went on to discuss mitosis while my imagination froze in the destruction to come.

Fifteen miles away, at the epicenter in Whittier, unreinforced brick buildings crumbled. A storefront fell onto a 1970s Honda Accord hatchback, the same kind my grandfather drove until we inherited it. The picture would appear in the news footage for days from different angles until the one car became thousands in my mind, cars just like ours suffocating under a chalky blanket of bricks, with me in the back seat, crushed.

Statistically, over 1,300 people in the LA area die every year from air pollution alone. These slow, suffocating deaths attract no news cameras or breaking headlines fraught with tense digital music. The victims die in hospital beds, not under concrete bridges. If 1,300 people died annually in earthquake-related injuries, the government would pour its money into infrastructure. Only six had died in the Whittier quake.

But as an anxious teenager, I had no interest in statistics or quantified suffering. I clung to the news to tell me everything would be okay. I didn't realize the news made money from doing exactly the opposite.

While stations continued to cover the Whittier quake,

stern-faced men in rolled-up shirt sleeves, rubble behind them, would warn, "This is not the Big One we've been waiting for for years. The Big One…[insert dramatic newscaster pause] …will be much worse." At that point, I began to learn about the Richter scale. The Whittier quake was a 5.9, while a 7.0 would be over one hundred times larger. An 8.0, what the Big One was supposed to be, one hundred times larger than that. I tried to multiply the destruction I saw on the TV by one thousand, the six deaths by one thousand, and could barely breathe.

Although our house sustained just a few shifted pictures on the wall, I convinced myself the Big One was nigh, most likely within a week or two; at the very latest, by the turn of the millennium. "I've got just ten years to live," I told my mom. She told me not to talk like that. I wasn't trying to be dramatic; I really believed it.

My mind shifted, cracked. I had trouble understanding why other people weren't paralyzed by this prediction, why they weren't fleeing for their lives for solid land in Arizona, Nevada. But they kept going. Built new houses, even. Didn't they know that an 8.0 would mean certain death for all but the luckiest southern Californians? Buildings–supposed places of shelter–became my enemy. Every time I walked into a room, I looked for where I would duck and cover, or, more likely, run for my life. I felt safe only when outside. During track meets I would sit in the middle of the field with a cup of Gatorade, look up at the open space with no power lines or trees, and think, "Now. Now would be the time. Can we just get it over with while I'm out here?"

Worry was a cognitive activity, but my dread of earthquakes had begun to take root in my body, in the feeling of dread in my stomach that made all food feel like a foreign body, in the adrenaline that sizzled in my fingertips. It was the beginning of an indelicate balance, trauma and anxiety mixing together and slowly carving grooves in my brain that would direct my thoughts and decisions. The coming Big One embodied my parents' unpredictable moods, the girl at school who kicked me in the shins, my fear of surprise that made me tell my future husband when and where he needed to propose, my eventual flight from California, the land responsible, or so I thought, for my fears.

The Big One still hasn't come. Southern California experiences a very large quake every 110-140 years, and it's been 160. My mother's brood of breakables has only increased since my childhood, joined by over two dozen miniature dollhouses she has constructed with intricate tweezers and knives. Light shines across the potted oranges on the patio through cut glass hangings that bend rainbows across the oriental rugs. She sleeps at odd hours, two cats in the crooks of her legs.

At any time, the faults could shift. Not just the San Andreas, but the Newport-Inglewood fault that runs right alongside my home town. At any time, those antique-bedecked walls could crumble or the grandfather clock could go smashing through the carved, cherry table covered with lace. It could happen any day, maybe even one of the two days out of the year I stay at my old house, chandelier swinging and shattering against the wall, the bridge to the 605 at the end of our street collapsing, my children clinging to me as I cling to my mother, crying, "This is where we're from."

~

I grew up at the convergence of two tectonic plates—the North American and Pacific. Did I not have a front-row seat to planetary history? My whole young life, while dreaming of flat, quiet fields, I lived and drove alongside and across one of the most dramatic boundaries on earth, holding my breath.

I lived on a burning Ring of Fire. The Ring traces a 25,000-mile volcano-dotted horseshoe of plate boundaries along the coasts of North and South America, the Bering Strait, Japan, and New Zealand. Ninety percent of the world's earthquakes occur on the ring.

As a kid, I'd watch news people interview residents of Malibu and Laguna, two glittering towns that seem to constantly be on fire or covered with mud.

"I wouldn't trade it for a thing," a woman in diamonds and Oakley sunglasses would inevitably respond to the question of "why here?" And most Californians would nod in enthusiastic agreement, perhaps buying a gallon or two of bottled water to prepare for their own community's impending disaster before swiftly forgetting their own daily fire walks over fault lines and drought belts.

North America *is* moving westward at three inches per year as the Pacific Plate with its fringe of coastal California, nudges up toward Alaska. Sometimes, if I sit very still on my midwestern front stoop, I can feel it, waving goodbye to my childhood as it drifts toward the Northern Lights.

~

Five months after the Northridge quake of 1994, at age 21, I moved to Ohio where nothing could harm me.

My new husband, Jeremy, and I graduated from college, packed the 16-year-old Honda Accord I had inherited from my grandfather, and drove to Bowling Green in Wood County, one of those coveted squarish counties in northwest Ohio. I'd decided to attend BGSU for an MFA in poetry after sorting through a number of possibilities in a number of states. I had not applied to even *one* program in the Golden State. Jeremy, ever faithful to his new, neurotic bride, agreed to the adventure of moving into a brick graduate apartment, sight unseen. He had no idea this would be the first year of two decades in the Midwest.

On the long trip inland, our car chugged through the Cajon Pass, overheating to the point that we had to pour water on the engine every few exits. We couldn't find a hotel within two hours of the Mojave desert because of a sold out Grateful Dead concert in Las Vegas, so we kept driving, until 5:30 am, where for $80 an Arizona motel let us sleep until 11am checkout. We passed through Route 66 for a couple more days until reaching the Texas panhandle, the flatness of the land opening like two huge fatherly hands. As we headed through Oklahoma, the Ozarks, and finally, the plains of Illinois and Indiana, my body relaxed into my seat. Silos. Water towers. Signs of a quiet life. Flat, unmoving earth underfoot.

The first time my husband and I visited California after our move to the Midwest, my dad picked us up from my father-in-law's house in Riverside to take us to his new home in the high desert town of Apple Valley. While I had seen many pictures of the sprawling ranch home he shared with his new wife, Judy, and a half-dozen dogs and cats, I'd never visited in person.

My dad drove, my husband sat in back, and I sat up front, where I could easily bear witness to my father's role as impresario of the Mojave Desert. As the 215 met up with the 15, and we headed into Cajon Pass, he announced that the "San Gabriel Mountains are on your right, San Bernardino on your left," a fact he repeated so many times, he ended up shortening it to "San Gabriel left, San Bernardino right," a catchphrase Jeremy and I would repeat for years to come. *San Gabriel, left, San Bernardino, right.*

The geography of my home state wasn't important to me, especially since I had no intention of returning. Hills and mountains and saints were everywhere, and my father's exacting descriptions turned into background noise as I tried to navigate my emotions veering to the edge of a 70-mph freeway.

Since my parents' divorce right before I left for college, I'd held back from him. I felt loyal to my mother. He'd been the one who left and did so cruelly, choosing to move out on their 21st wedding anniversary, telling her she had to stay locked up in the back room as he marched around with boxes.

My mom had paid my way through college, reminding me constantly that *she* was carrying the burden. I was stuck between not wanting to upset her, and not wanting to upset him, but being the good daughter—the one who should honor my mother and father, even if I didn't honor their personalities or decisions. Honoring him meant visiting, staying neutral, not bringing up anything too tender or too scary.

It was my first time back to California in two years. We

had put off visiting long enough. A grad assistant and construction workers' income didn't make plane tickets the easiest to afford, although I couldn't say what was the bigger driver: I had flown just once, as a high school senior, and had developed a terror of planes. I didn't want *anything* to blow up: parents, cars, planes, my own fears.

I sat quietly in the front seat, nodding and following the pointing finger. As the landscape began to barren out a little more and the elevation rose to over three thousand feet, my ears popping, I pointed to some sharp rocks jutting stegosauruslike just west of the freeway. "So what are those?" I asked, happy I had finally found a way to reciprocate interest.

"Those? Oh, those are rock formations. Pushed up by the San Andreas fault."

"The San Andreas fault? *The San Andreas?*"

"Yeah. It's right there on the side of the freeway."

He spoke offhandedly, as if pointing out the local Kmart. I knew the fault was out there somewhere. It was mythical. Capable of great destruction but also invisible in some way, like God.

I stared at the ancient, rain-pocked sandstone. I tried to imagine what it would be like to drive alongside the fault when the Big One struck. To be anywhere in SoCal during the Big One would be dramatic. But to be right there, to sink, fly? Slide into the core of the earth?

"Are...you scared to live that close to the fault?"

"Scared? No. When the Big One hits, we'll be on the North American side, not the Pacific side. They'll do all the shaking."

Somehow, I knew that was a line high-desert dwellers told themselves, but I let it go. Property was cheap in the stark, triple-digit land of the high desert. "Desert rats" had to sell themselves on the safety and appeal of the place, or at least that's what I thought before I started to get a weakness for barren expanses punctuated with rocks.

The longer I stared at those formations, the more I convinced myself the San Andreas would give way. Now. Anxiety can be so narcissistic, leading the anxious one to believe her very presence is enough to crash cars, plunge planes, and activate faults.

After learning about the fault's proximity to the Cajon Pass, I would hold my breath every time we drove to my father's house, as if it made a difference whether I was two, ten, or twenty miles away from one of the largest, most infamous faults in the world. I started to resent the fact that I had to cross a chasm in order to visit my father. Passing into the land of my dad, a desert that seemed so fragilely perched atop such uneven land. A place where a gun was in the drawer and he bragged about it. Where everything seemed to be on the brink of exploding. Traveling across the freeway that shone like cracked black leather, I would will myself back to the flat suburban Chicago highways two thousand miles away.

The subject of those freeway rocks came up later as I processed difficult memories in therapy. Although nothing had actually happened to me at the rocks, they broke through my mind every time I thought of California, until they became as iconic as the state flag's shaggy bear. I had to pry them from that deep place in my body, had to put them to rest.

First, I learned they had a name: the Mormon Rocks,

named for the Mormon settlers who traveled to California in covered wagons on their way to founding the city of San Bernardino. The rocks provided shade for the exhausted sojourners; what I saw as danger was a place of refuge. There was an interpretive trail, just one mile long, through the sandstone formations. I knew what I had to do when I visited California in the future.

So on my next visit, after spending time with my dad and Judy, a pleasant couple of days spent watching Doris Day movies and going out to Steer and Stein restaurant, where the waitresses sang *Phantom of the Opera* with my dad, I hit the road "back down the hill," as the Hi-Des dwellers call it when crossing into LA, Orange County, and the rest of the doomed Pacific Plate.

As I exited their driveway, I waved and watched Dad and Judy wave back in the rearview mirror, arm in arm by the Joshua tree. We follow this ritual every time I leave, and every time I feel guilty, knowing I'm the one who left and wondering if this is the last time I'll see them alive. I wound my way through desert streets and the massively congested Bear Valley Road, grabbed a coffee to reward myself for being a good daughter, got on the 15, and exited on 138 toward Palmdale. I drove just a mile, and pulled into the Mormon Rocks Fire Station, where the trail begins.

Wisteria clambered over fences in innocent splendor. The station seemed empty, just a car or two in the lot. I wanted to knock on the door and introduce myself as one who had finally dared to enter their world, a world as everyday to them as my coffee pot and dog routine is to me. I wanted to ask if they saw their office space of fault rocks and railroads as a hall of horrors.

I followed the "TRAIL" sign toward the start of the interpretive trail which apparently had no interpreter, brochures, or signs. Just a rattlesnake warning and numbered markers on a one-mile loop among the rocks and wildflowers. So I quickly gave up any illusion of learning about my surroundings and instead allowed them to surround me. I was the only person on the trail.

I had not expected so much vegetation, but right away I found myself winding through clouds of wooly sunflower, bending down to touch orange mariposa lilies. The petals of purple statice stuck to my sandals and toes like flecks of nail polish. It was easy to get drawn into the fleeting lives of these plants while forgetting what I came for: the geography of my mind.

When I looked up, I found myself standing at the bottom of a high-desert postcard of color and shadow, a cobalt sky veiled with cirrus clouds that would occasionally drift and thicken over the sun, providing a moment of dusk until the sun blazed again. These clouds held the power of obscurity, dark as smoke, shadowing the jagged tops of the Mormon rocks that now, seen for the first time from land and not the freeway, held a certain inevitability. They couldn't *not* be there, as strange as they were, and the ground beneath them deserved its chance to move. Standing on a ridge above the most famous fault in the world, perched above the Ring of Fire, I felt smaller and larger than ever before.

Near the end of my journey, I took time to go off-trail and walk up to one of the Mormon Rocks and place my hand against it. As far as rocks go, this was like cotton candy–malleable, dissolving in the rain. But it was also 18 million years old, pushed up by the San Andreas. I took a picture of my hand on the sandstone–short fingers that looked odd on my tall body.

I stood breathing slowly, palm to my fear, then picked up a small stone that had rolled off the rock and put it in my pocket, where its seismic pulses would run through my hands. I would carry it in my purse for a year and not take it out until going through security at Six Flags Great America.

"What's this?" the security guy asked, taking the rock out of my purse after he searched it with a stick.

I explained my hike, the fault, the meaning of the rock. He didn't care.

"I won't throw it at anyone, if that's what you're wondering," I said. "I never take it out of my purse."

He handed it back, raising his eyebrow enough to let me know I had better not give a thought to hurling it at the upside-down riders on the Demon.

I avoided rides that day, like I do every time I visit. As my family flung themselves through the atmosphere, I watched children hit their siblings with empty cotton candy cones. I stared at complicated scaffoldings holding up roller coasters and lost myself in the angles and shadows, equally mesmerized and numbed by the way we humans pass the time. I ran my fingers over the surface of my San Andreas stone as the people on the Superman coaster screamed through their rumbling ride, dreading and loving the danger they sought.

FREEWAYS

When Jeremy and I moved to the Chicago area in the 1990s, we were teased for the way we asked for directions: "What's the fastest way to get downtown? The 294 or the 94? Or should we take the 90?"

"'What's with all the *the's*?" our friends responded. "It's just I-94."

It took us a year or so, but we eventually learned to say the highway numbers and drop the articles until visiting our native California, where we tacked the *the's* back on.

Nowadays, most people know that southern Californians are famous for saying *the* in front of freeway numbers. It's been analyzed, written about, and heavily satirized on SNL's parody soap opera, *The Californians*. There's a simple explanation for this dialect. The first freeway in the West, connecting Pasadena to Los Angeles, was called The Arroyo Seco Parkway. Soon other freeways came to the area, such as The Hollywood and The San Diego. Once the rest of the country started to catch up with highway construction, designating most of them with numbers, California made the switch to numbers, too. However, Angelenos were so used to using articles, they never dropped the *the's*. Hence, Interstate 405, for example, became "the 405."

But I like to think the *the's* mean so much more. In Southern California, freeways are entities in themselves that loom, quite literally, in residents' everyday lives. In fact, the anthropomorphic power of freeways makes me wonder if they deserve to be called "Ms. 57" or "Daddy 605."

Freeways are presences, not just numbers, in the mythology of the Golden State. As Kevin Starr, California historian writes, "the challenge of designing freeways...constituted an art form growing in complexity....As in the case of all great engineering on such a monumental scale, the freeways bespoke the values and technology, the options and choices, the sheer drama, of the brave new world Californians were creating."

And the freeways *are* sheer drama: four-level interchanges built boldly above fault lines, sweeping their godlike arms over the suburban megalopolis—a pure, unbroken succession of palm trees, malls, and big-box stores butting up against soundproof walls.

It didn't take long for these emblems of freedom to morph into symbols of crowding, pollution, and rage. Californians hate and utterly devote themselves to their freeways, practically living in the cars that convey them from one fraught, sunny destination to another.

Years ago, my older sister told me about a several-hours-long traffic backup on The 91, an East-West freeway that covers roughly sixty miles from Gardena to Riverside. It was a summer day in the 80s, back when probably just half the cars had air conditioning. As traffic crawled westward among the canyons and valleys of Corona and Yorba Linda, irritable commuters prayed for the inevitable construction cones or sheeted bodies to finally appear on the shoulder so they could get the hell on with their lives.

This time there *were* two bodies, bodies that were very much alive. Two teenage girls waiting to get help for their broken-down car had decided to take advantage of the sunny downtime. They lay out on the roof of their car in bikinis, oblivious, or perhaps proud, of the traffic jam that simultaneously ruined and made people's days, some men bringing their cars to a standstill and placing them in park.

It was as SoCal as you can get: cars and bathing suits backgrounded by smog-covered Jack-in-the-Box signs in the hills. A laid-back life in theory punctuated by the cursing of thousands of people crossing hours of deserts and fault lines to get to the homes they could barely afford.

Ana Sanchez, a playwright living in Long Beach, describes the freeways this way:

> I see them as demigods. If you're in SoCal, they can make or break your day. They rule your schedule, your planning, and your worldview moment-to-moment. They can make you see others as less than human, worthy of insults and curses heaped upon them. They lead you past cities you may never enter, giving you glimpses of what you were, or what you could have been. They separate us, and also unite us in our communal sacrifice of time and space to get to other places. They rule us and have more power over us than we like to admit, and we are always at their mercy.

Joan Didion, in a similar manner, calls "the freeway system... the only secular communion Los Angeles has." Even though every state in the union has at least one major freeway or interstate within its borders, the California highway system takes on a whole other dimension. While I lived on those highways as a student in the early 90s, people flirted across lanes and traded phone numbers in traffic jams. Middle fingers escalated into fatal altercations. Razor wire kept gang members from tagging exit signs, while communities collaborated on underpass murals. Driving on the freeway in California was about the individual—the mountain, beach and desert traveler with tinted windows, booming music, and an In-N-Out Burger bumper sticker snipped neatly to read "In-N-Out Urge." It was the shared communal sacrifice of individualism, derived from the terrible freedom of owning a car, a dream, and someplace to go.

As a child, I didn't spend much time on the freeways. My dad didn't enjoy visiting places, and my mom nurtured an extreme phobia of driving at high speeds. She'd only go on the freeway as a passenger, and not without constantly pressing a phantom brake pedal into the floorboards whenever another car changed lanes.

When still in her twenties, my mother and her second husband had rolled their Plymouth Fury off an embankment on a Utah highway. While lying there among the scattered suitcases and clothes with gasoline in her hair, she heard people exclaim, "They've gotta be dead!"

She and her husband crawled to life and hitched a ride back down to California without going to the doctor. My mom refused to drive on a freeway ever again, taking surface streets all over the greater Orange County and Los Angeles areas, even if that meant driving through the "undesirable" neighborhoods the freeways conveniently skip by.

In my high school driver's ed class, Mr. Schwandt wasted little time getting us out on The 605 freeway that ran near Los

Alamitos. I was in a car with three other students, one of them a popular girl named Pamela. I had done fine on the driving simulators, but my two times behind the wheel so far had felt out of body, the blue Corolla like the inside of my head with a cold: big, wobbly, and caught in a tunnel where breath was scarce. Mostly, I didn't want to face the dire social repercussions for killing Pam.

Taking the Cerritos Avenue onramp, with its slow curve around the ice plant flowers, felt like I was being slowly unfurled into space, like an astronaut on a tether. When it was finally time to merge onto the freeway, my speedometer quivered at 20.

"Step on the gas!" Mr. Schwandt barked.

As the cars rushed in behind and around me, I took my foot off the pedal completely and pictured us tumbling over the embankment, gasoline in Pamela's beach-bleached hair.

"Speed up! Come on!" he yelled, and in the rearview I caught the kids in the backseat smirking. Then, as more cars started swerving and honking, they started yelling, "Go, go go!" as well.

When I finally got the courage to accelerate, I saw a semi coming up behind us and immediately slammed on the brakes. The kids in the backseat screamed.

"Tania, you can't slam on the brakes on the freeway," the teacher said, as my hands trembled obediently at 10 and 2 on the wheel. "This is The 605!"

"Sorry. Sorry. Sorry," I mumbled, glazed with tears. I eventually made it to 35 mph, hazards on, and exited quietly at the next ramp.

Yet. The 605. I had done it terribly, but I had done it, directed four wheels down the same road thousands of other wheels would touch that day on their way to malls and LA office buildings and the Hollywood sidewalk stars I still hadn't seen. For a moment, I was less than human: a Californian who couldn't drive. The other kids' worldview that day? Tania sucks. Yet I had had my moment on the rim of the portal.

My behind-the-wheel hours resulted in several more embarrassing incidents involving curb-clipping turns that tipped us to the side and some harrowing lefts on red. Once Mr. Schwandt called me a "hazard to society," and it didn't take long before the whole sophomore class heard.

I would find out later that my mom called the school—something she had never done before since I was a straight-A student—and talked the teacher into letting me pass so we could complete the California permit process. Eventually I'd fail my first driver's test, passing the second time with the minimum score.

But with that skin-of-my-teeth card, I had my Disney E-ticket to freedom, The Freedom to roll down the windows of my grandfather's 78 Honda Accord, curve around the concrete multi-level interchanges, and take off as the shadows of eucalyptus leaves played in my hair. In time, I got better: faster, more confident, and able to negotiate merges with ease. My mom marveled as she rode in the passenger seat, phantom-braking just once in awhile.

"Look what you can do," she said, and shook her head.

David Brodsky, who wrote "L.A. Freeway: An Appreciative Essay" in 1981, notes, "the freeway allows you to create your own life. Your community is formed not by geography or community but by common interests."

For the next couple of years, these common interests would take me to shopping malls and beaches. In college, they would take me to classical concerts and chamber music rehearsals. Eventually, they would take me to boyfriends' houses and fiancé's relatives. They would take me on The 15 straight through San Bernardino, Barstow, and Baker, then straight on out of the Golden State, my husband and I disappearing into the asphalt mirage.

~

So much depends upon August 4, 1990, the Saturday I celebrated my 18th birthday. Though I don't have a picture, I assume I wore a cropped floral T-shirt and high-waisted acid-washed shorts.

My parents and I had finished visiting my sister Heidi's house to celebrate my birthday. She and her family had recently purchased land in Temecula, a rural community in Riverside County that would increase in population by three hundred percent over the next few decades. The drive usually took just an hour and fifteen minutes, but the sparsely developed country roads made the trip seem exotic and otherworldly.

I curled my long legs into the back seat of the Accord and watched the brown hillsides glide by on our way to Orange County. After passing through Santa Ana Canyon between Corona and Yorba Linda and then funneling into the tighter lanes through Anaheim and Fullerton, drivers can stay on the 91 headed west or veer to the right to take the 5 north toward Los Angeles. We had to stay on 91 to eventually pick up the 605, but my father got distracted, stayed to the right, and followed the 5.

"Shit!" he yelled. "I missed it!" Our car began to curve into the hinterlands of Buena Park, past the exit to Beach Boulevard and Knott's Berry Farm. "Dammit!"

My mom straightened her back and clenched the door handle. Her red bushy hair trembled.

"It's not a big deal, Hal. Just get off the next exit."

"Shut up! It *is* a big deal!" he shouted. My heart plunged to my feet. Dad slammed his fist on the dashboard. I couldn't stop the yelp that escaped from my mouth.

"Shut up!" he yelled again, eyes darting to the rearview mirror, and struck the top of the steering wheel with the heel of his hand. The car lurched to the left. We were going seventy miles per hour.

"Please," I pleaded with him quietly. "Please don't let us die."

"Fuck!" he responded, and punched the dash. "I can't believe I missed it!" He hit the dash harder, enough to make a blast of sound that caused me to hold my ears and start crying.

"Hal!" my mother yelled. "Stop it!"

"No! No! No! It's not right! The whole ride home is now not right! Taking the 5 is wrong!"

He started hitting the steering wheel repeatedly, and we began to swerve, first within the lane, then across lanes. Cars and big rigs honked, my face just inches from a semi wheel.

My mom slammed down her right foot on the fake brake.

My dad let out an enormous sigh then suddenly righted the wheel, stared straight ahead, and kept driving. My mom started to say something, but I kicked the seat. *Don't talk,* I pleaded with her in my head. *You'll make him mad again.*

It wasn't that my dad was lost. It's that he did something wrong, something not according to plan. When it came to driving, exactitude was crucial. He reset his odometer every time we left the house to make sure the mile count was consistent. He would criticize me for saying a destination was "thirty minutes away." "That means nothing!" he would bark. "Distance is measured in miles!"

Eventually the interchange to the 22 appeared, which we then exited to head south toward the 405, the alternate way home. My dad fell silent, as did my mom and me, when we began to recognize familiar street names. Still, I gripped the gray cloth of the backseat until we exited at Seal Beach Boulevard.

After just a half mile or so, he pulled into our local shopping center, and my mom handed me a $10 bill. "Run into Lucky's and buy ice cream and M&Ms," she said. "For your birthday."

Three years later, when I wrote a ten-page letter to my father explaining why I didn't want him to give me away at my wedding, I cataloged the freeway scene as a touchstone I kept returning to when reflecting on our relationship. He didn't remember.

For many years in my adult life, I insisted on taking the wheel on freeways. Even with my husband, a very cautious driver, I thought I would die without complete control. If something was going to happen, an explosive, action-movie crash, it was going to be because of me, and only me, so I wouldn't have to fear betrayal. I needed the feel of the hot steering wheel in one hand, the gearshift in the other. I wouldn't even drive an automatic transmission because of the perceived lack of control, the road unspooling like a ribbon on which I was sliding and flying.

~

Jeremy and I moved to the Midwest a week after the OJ Simpson car "chase" (the speed never topped 60 mph) drew the nation to their TV screens. As OJ hid in the backseat of his friend's Bronco on the 405 from Orange County to LA, Jeremy and I packed the smallest U-Haul trailer we could find, hooked it to the back of the Accord, and headed east on the 15 and 40 until the land flattened out.

At a gas station, we bought a couple gallons of water to pour on the overheating engine. We also picked up a discounted Journey cassette from the early 80s.

All two thousand miles, the first song, "Any Way You Want It," was the one we heard the most, every time we popped it into the dusty deck to start over. The *she* in the song was a she who loves everything. A she open to adventure, window rolled down, hair blowing. Your typical California babe, not an anxious girl curled up in the backseat of memory with a mind of death.

The eventual release into the open fields of Ohio set me joyously spinning. In a matter of months I drank in the humidity and fireflies of summer evenings, pressed colored leaves between the pages of books, and built snowmen in front of our brick apartment. I was a child, starting life over while working on Masters-level projects. This was my freedom, except when memory brought me back to seasonless

California's shadowy clutch of mountains, an angry ocean whipping the shore.

A quarter of a century after my 18th birthday and two decades after leaving California, I decided to take it on: the PTSD that shadowed me. The therapist calls me back to the 91/5 interchange. I'm in the backseat. My dad pounds the dash, car swerving. I track the movement of the Eye Movement Desensitization and Reprocessing light, a green dot bouncing back and forth across a black electronic bar.

"Go to where you are," the therapist says. "What do you feel?"

"He's scaring me."

"Use 'I' statements."

"I'm scared. I'm out of control. I can't save myself."

A chilly autumn day in Illinois, I'm in the sweltering backseat surrounded by hillsides and Del Taco drive-thrus baking in the smog. I breathe. I imagine myself safe. I *was* safe. I *am* safe.

"I'm going to be okay. I'm going to make it," I say.

~

My California suburb was hemmed in by two freeways, The 405 and The 605. Because of relatives who settled inland and my eventual attendance at the University of California, Riverside, I often found myself traveling east-west from The 91 to The 605. To reach my house, I exited at Katella Avenue, which is a major street that passes through Orange County from Los Alamitos to the city of Orange. Disneyland is its most famous address. The Rea family, who settled in Anaheim as walnut farmers in 1896, named the rural path in front of their farm Katella Road after their two daughters, Kate and Ella. The two girls playing under the shade of walnut trees could not imagine their namesake becoming a major thoroughfare of malls, car chases, flipped motorcycles, and border patrol arrests.

To the left of the Katella exit runs a steep concrete bed for the channelized San Gabriel River that empties into the Pacific at Seal Beach. As a teenager, I rode my bike on this wall all the way to the ocean and thought nothing about the mountains that supplied that skinny stream 43 miles away.

Inside the curve is a huge bed of what I now, in a fit of nostalgia, think is the most beautiful flower in the world: ice plant, otherwise known as freeway plant. When you drive the California freeways, you see millions of these succulents with yellow and magenta blossoms. It turns out they are invasive, just like the freeways they line.

Southern California is all about invasion. The invasion of people, concrete, and now, even the flowers I thought were home. But perhaps it wouldn't be wrong for me to consider them California plants. Even native. We grew up together, the ice plant and I. Before I had even *heard* of the cape of South Africa, their original home, I had imprinted them in the same sensory mix of Beach Boys music, orange rinds, and Coppertone mixed with sand.

But the flowers that were supposed to save the landscape have ruined it. They've caused landslides they were intended to prevent. Other plants that should live here, the various coastal scrub and chaparral, have been choked out by the color and glitz.

Typical of California. Dreams become dangerous. Beach

houses require living in neighborhoods planted with "TSUNAMI ZONE" signs that portray white stick figures running from encroaching waves. Find that perfect suburb, then escape it. Keep moving, away from the floods, away from the smog. Go east, south, away from the danger. When the immigrants come, get out. Go to Nevada. When that bottom drops out, Texas. Lose money. Lots of it. Try to go back to the beach with the tsunami sign and realize you can't even afford to rent a garage.

What *is* the real California, and can it ever be found? Aren't the highway plants like the rest of us who found ourselves part of the big, golden problem on the edge of the world?

I learn that ice plant can be eaten, the flowers made into a jam, the leaves steeped as a tea. I want to try it, ingest California, or, more precisely, South Africa-become-California, and let it enter my bloodstream. Sunshine and exhaust in a cup.

This past summer, sitting in traffic on The 405 as my mom and family made our way down to Venice beach, I saw plenty of tempting buds of freeway plant carpeting the littered shoulder.

"You could probably hop out and grab some now," my Mom said, but I felt too scared to get out of my car, the crazy gal in a rusty minivan with Illinois plates breaking who knows how many laws by flying out of her car and ripping a plant from the side of a major thoroughfare.

But I couldn't leave California without taking some back to the Midwest. On our last day in Orange County, the last time we would exit The 605 to the neighborhood of my childhood before gradually heading East and North, I grabbed my husband's shoulder.

"Pull over!"

"Right here?" We had just come off that curve of ice plant on the busy Eastbound rush Katella.

"Yes, hurry!" He pulled over, turned on his hazards, and said we'd probably get a ticket.

I ran along the shoulder and yanked out a clump. I had never touched it before, and it was sticky and crawling with bugs. I jumped back in the car and tossed it on the console.

My mother eyed the ice plant nervously as I rinsed the bugs off in her garage sink and sealed it in a plastic bag. "Don't let those bugs in my garden!" she warned. I tucked it away in the box of medicines and toiletries I packed for our month on the road and forgot about it.

Four weeks after leaving Orange County, I remembered my plan to taste the non-native plant of my native land and decided to brew some tea. I would chop up the leaves, which would have surely dried by now, and let them infuse the water with their salty-sour-sweet essence.

When I pulled the bag out of my bottom drawer, I did not find dried, shriveled leaves. The succulents had stayed plump but gray and moldy. Evidently, rinsing them at my mother's house and then storing them in a plastic bag had done its damage. I threw them in the trash having learned nothing except for the difficulty of forcing epiphanies from symbolic gestures.

~

Sometimes my parents drove north, sailing right through LA on the way up to Solvang, a Danish tourist town hemmed in by windmills, souvenir shops, and statues of Hans Christian Andersen. We took the 5, that ventricle of highway that eventually pulses right up to the Canadian border, then the 101 winding languidly along the Santa Barbara coast.

I lay in the backseat of our silver Corolla, waiting for the cats to appear.

The LA River, which runs 51 miles from the San Fernando Valley to the Pacific Ocean, was surrounded by a concrete flood control channel in 1938 as a response to the loss of life and property that came with the rare, but heavy, rains. Some have described the river as "straightjacketed," stripped of its natural banks and habitat and forced into a channel portholed with storm drains. To me, those drains were magic.

The drain covers, heavy metal circles several feet in diameter, connect to the concrete river bank with triangular hinges that resemble cat ears. Starting in the 1960s, graffiti artists began applying paint to these covers, suggesting feline faces.

In the late 70s, the cats were mostly black and white, reminiscent of Felix but displaying a variety of features and personalities: whiskers, winks, grins, frowns, and surprised mouths. As quickly as I spotted the cats, I lost them in the northward rush. The only child in that backseat, I cultivated a private world that understood the necessity of making cat faces out of drains.

Traveling anywhere with my parents was a rare excursion into the known unknown. Driving more than fifteen minutes meant an oil change and tire pressure check, hours of poring over maps. Would my parents fight? Would my father say something embarrassing, complain about the price of a beer, or leer at a woman? The car was the best and worst place to be, especially if the classical radio was on and my parents weren't talking, and the cats and I made eye contact for a moment.

I found my way into anthropomorphic companionship in my backyard as well. Inspired by *Love Boat,* I likened the roar of the 605 freeway that ran behind my house to the raging ocean, my whole backyard, the ship. I didn't take romantic escapades with handsome strangers down to Puerto Vallarta. I floated on the water without a destination. I stuffed magnolia grandiflora leaves with twigs and flower petals and called them tacos. I spun fuchsia blossoms in buckets of water like synchronized swimmers and called them on-deck entertainment. My business was more than just looking for faces. I created an entire ship of metaphors, poetry as a way of keeping myself company. I created a richer life than what was there and stored it up.

As a child, I didn't understand my local geography—its mountains, rivers, and infrastructure. I didn't know LA even had a technical river, just a slab of concrete over a stream of brown water as seen through the window-world of the car. I liked to think the cats appeared mysteriously in the middle of the night.

Turns out, human fingerprints were all over them.

In the 1960s, a woman named Jackie Meyer and her husband biked to the Atwater River area to paint cats on the storm drains. Leo Limon, inspired when he spotted the cats on his way to a school trip to the LA Zoo, began painting the cats himself in 1970, eventually adding color and flair with spray paint cans.

Even after being drafted to Vietnam and having three children, Limon continued his training among other East LA Latino artists. He took a job with Self Help Graphics, a printmaking studio committed to helping youth express themselves. Now he builds awareness to the natural and cultural importance of the LA River. Although he has received permits for the cats over the years, he finds them painted over as a result of graffiti abatement programs. In fact, during our correspondence over email, when I remarked I'd like to see the cats again, he told me to save my gas.

In his community, an erased cat face is an erased piece of identity. As a girl in a walled suburb, who only passed through LA to get to other white tourist towns, I didn't—couldn't—perceive the cats as communal objects. The homeless who lived by the river? Invisible to me. The Latino communities? Almost as invisible. In fact, it wasn't until a decade after my high school graduation that I opened my senior yearbook and noticed the faces captioned with names like Rodriguez and Ruiz. Where were they? Why didn't I know them? They lived in another part of town, took different classes, and ate lunch on another part of campus.

Likewise, the cat faces entertained me, a rush of ears and whiskers on my way to the Danish pastries and miniature wooden clocks that would convince me, at least for the hour of purchase, that our family enjoyed spending time together. From the freeway, the cats were as small as a row of bottle caps. East LA children, on the other hand, biked or walked right up to them, crunching the leaves that rustled into the concrete corners. They stretched their arms to reach the span of the ears, stood eye to eye with the smudged pupils.

Despite Leo's warning, I wanted to venture down to the riverbed myself to try to find the cats. On a scalding June day during one of my brief visits to my childhood home, I shared my strange intentions with my mother, and she volunteered to come along. I was surprised by her sense of adventure. Driving into East LA to walk on a riverbed, an 81-year-old woman and her 44-year-old daughter?

When I saw my mom pull her floppy hat and sunscreen shirt out of the closet, I realized she would also be risking dehydration. Known for drinking six or seven cups of a coffee a day with little to no water to balance them, my mother had passed out several times in the past few years.

"Mom, we'll be walking in the hot sun. You need water!"

"I'm okay," she said, tucking a tiny bottle of Aquafina in her fanny pack. I suspected she wouldn't drink a drop.

I typed "Atwater Village," the access point to the river cats, into Google Maps and wasn't surprised to see that one of the mythical lands from my childhood was only 30 miles away, just east of Hollywood.

The drive would take us up the 605 to the 5. Auto malls, overpasses, industrial buildings. Cars waiting to move; people waiting to live. Signs for Downey, Pico Rivera, and Montebello. East LA.

As we approached our exit, I looked to the right, the same place where I had always turned my head as a child to exchange glances with the cats. The drain covers were faceless.

I knew I was wrong but held out some hope anyway:

"Maybe if we exit here and park, we can take the river walk and find a cat." The thought of bringing the far up close, as much as it would fall short of the ideal, sent a little thrill to my fingertips as I signaled.

We exited onto Los Feliz Ave. and pulled into the municipal park, where we could leave our car and walk to the gate that would lead us to the concrete path above the LA River. My mother took her time in the parking lot adjusting her hat and pulling a long-sleeved sun shirt over her pale, freckled arms. It was late morning, already over 90 degrees.

As we approached the sidewalk congested with midday lunch goers, I began to frame my disappointment for the up-close encounter with those whitewashed, empty faces and ears. I would have to write about how things can never be the same, how my childhood, for better or worse, vanished with those wild faces as the neighborhood gentrified to the seven-dollar-cup-of-Chemex-coffee level.

In less than 60 seconds, we had arrived at a tall iron gate called Guardians of the River. Designed by Michael Amescua, an LA artist who integrates imagery from Pre-Columbian myth and ritual into his iron work, the gate resembles a menagerie of shadow puppets. A sun with fiery spires fills the arch above the gate, and beneath that frolic iron cut-outs of a deer, a heron, a puma, a lemur-like creature. I had not expected these animals on our walk.

"Look at that gate!" My mom exclaimed. "It's so arty."

"Arty" was the highest compliment my mother could give. "Pretty" means boring and mainstream. "Unusual" indicates poor taste. But "arty" encompasses uniqueness, whimsy, and high-class eccentricity.

Throughout her life, my mother rarely gave herself the authority to say no to her abusers or to her fears, but when it came to creativity and design, she was the ultimate authority. She decorated my sixth-grade locker with remnant carpet squares and antique-printed wallpaper samples while other girls hung up posters of Duran Duran. She turned my school dioramas into fanciful scenes from books she never read as I did nothing more than color in a mom-cut birch tree, helpless as her enthusiasm for scissors and rubber cement took over.

While art projects stressed me out, my mom told me that my drawings were, indeed, arty, and that I was even artier with stories and words. While she spent seven years hand-stitching a quilt that belonged in the Met rather than a country gift store, I kept myself alive in my quirky worlds whose primitive illustrations were means to psychological ends. Hello Kitty and Garfield made money. The River Catz, like the animals in my books, made sense. And now the Guardians.

The arty gate, littered at the base with fast-food wrappers, was padlocked shut.

"Well. So much for that," I said.

As we turned back, my mom pointed out a homemade footpath going up the side of the embankment by the parking lot. It appeared to be blocked off with a flimsy plastic orange net, but we couldn't be entirely sure without ascending it. My mom took a chug of water to show she was serious. She hiked up her jeans and I followed, ready to climb.

"Hey!" I heard from behind us. I figured it had to be directed toward us, but then again, we were 81- and 44-year-old women. He whistled. I didn't turn around.

"Hey! Don't go up there!" A young Latino man in khakis stepped out from the small municipal golf course that bordered the parking lot. "It's closed off!"

As we approached him, I tried to stay casual. "I'm sorry, but I'm writing a book," I said, as if flashing a badge and announcing I was with the FBI. "Do you remember the cat faces?"

He shook his head. "A fence means they don't want you up there. They're redoing the river."

"Oh, okay, now," my mom said.

"But I don't live nearby. I came two thousand miles to see it."

He wasn't impressed. "Try getting to the river from somewhere else."

I knew I wouldn't.

BURBS

My first memory takes place in Lakewood, CA, a small suburb south of Los Angeles. Lakewood, the nation's first planned community, also happens to be the subject of D. J. Waldie's *Holy Land: A Suburban Memoir*. "In a suburb that is not exactly middle class," Waldie writes, "the necessary illusion is predictability."

Because the families that settle there are anything but.

My mom and dad bought one of those small, square dream homes from my father's parents in 1969. It was my dad's first marriage and my mother's third. Heidi, my sister born during one of my mother's prior lives, was in junior high.

On August 4, 1972, I was born a California girl. My mother was 36, her pregnancy considered high risk back then. According to her lore, I was supposed to be born disabled or dead. By some glorious twist of fate, I made it: long, skinny, and bald, but alive. I cried constantly, carrying my parents' DNA of anxiety and voluble self-expression.

In my first memory, I am younger than two. I know this because shortly before my second birthday we moved eight miles west to Rossmoor, the first walled community in the country, a town with posh British names and white concrete driveways and jacaranda trees dropping their blue blossoms on the sidewalks.

I emailed my dad about the Maybank address. I wanted to search for the house on Google Earth, maybe do a drive-by on my next trip out west. He said he couldn't remember the number, but he did remember that when he and my mom got back from their honeymoon, ready to move in, his parents still hadn't left. He had to stand in the middle of the room and demand that they get out, now, and go to their apartment. "I finally stood up to them like a man," he wrote.

My father is over 80. I don't remember his admitting to weaknesses very often. And making demands is usually one of his specialties. But for some reason, this story saddens me. I picture him standing in a room crowded with my mother's boxed antiques, ten years younger than I am now. Tall, thick, pointing a finger at his stern Ukrainian mother and hapless Austrian father.

He emailed again, a few days later: "I remember the number. 4547. I looked it up on Google Earth. Someone's added a bay window." And that was all he wanted to say.

Now that I had the address of my first home, I didn't want to search for it. I'm simultaneously drawn to and repelled by my past in the land jokingly referred to as North Disneyland, the border of Long Beach and Orange County. I've lived in the Midwest since grad school, safe from the earthquakes and smog and cars whizzing along the 91.

"But you have tornadoes out there," people say. "And Chicagoans drive like maniacs."

But for years I've insisted it's different, and figuring out why has become my work. So I eventually typed in the address and watched Google Earth spin: North America, then California, then Lakewood and Maybank Avenue racing toward me.

There was the neat street grid. Treetops. Roofs. The red location pin dropped.

In my first memory, I'm crawling on the floor and peering up at a large white wicker hamper. This is no laundry hamper. It's a container for all my toys.

I can't reach the lid, and I still haven't learned to walk. I can't even pull myself up to stand. So I look up at the white woven tower that holds all my joy. And reach.

As I pull down the hamper, the bright plastic colors of toys spill around me. But the toys themselves aren't enough. I need to reach the source, to live where the toys live. I crawl inside, curl up among bright rattles and balls.

It's the only thing I remember about 4547 Maybank. And now, as I select Street View, I prepare myself to approach the front door.

I like to think there's some meaning to that memory, my first quest for independence and safety. That quest has defined my life. Marrying young, moving far away, then surrounding myself with beauty on my own terms because I fear conflict, discomfort, pain. Even now I wrap myself in blankets on the hottest of summer days.

The screen shifts to Street View, but now I can't locate 4547 on the screen. The image jumps from one house to the next, and I find myself bouncing between the same white truck and palm tree of two different houses. I can't pinpoint 4547 after several minutes of trying. How did my father find the bay window? Did he? Then why can't I? I emailed him about my conundrum, but he didn't respond. He'd already moved on to other things.

Several months later, during a visit to California, I asked my mother and sister to do a drive-by with me. I was shocked when my mother, who rarely likes to leave her house, and who does not necessarily feel sentimental about life with my dad in the 1970s, complied.

The mythical Maybank house is only 9.5 miles from the Rossmoor home, and would take only 21 minutes to reach.

The neighborhood looks just as Waldie describes it: uniform, predictable, 46 houses per block. I would be dishonest if I said there wasn't something comforting about that perfect grid. Drought has pushed homeowners to forsake lawns for dirt and succulents, but even those neat squares of loss are beautiful. "It is as if each house on your block stood on its own enchanted island, fifty feet wide by one hundred feet long," writes Waldie.

When we turned onto Maybank, my sister's memories of her early teen years became mine as well. There was the sleepover in which one of her friends mimicked an exotic dancer, holding a candle beneath her breasts—and my dad, who apparently had watched the whole thing, lighting a match and mimicking her at breakfast. There was my mother walking out the door with newborn me so she could drive around the neighborhood for hours. "I need to sleep," he had told her. "No crying babies allowed." These stories would become my history.

"Slow down," my mom said, as I turned from Centralia onto Maybank. "It's going to be down here on the left."

"Is it here?" I put on the brake and edged my way along the curb.

"Hold on," Heidi said, then, "Wow. There it is. Wow."

"That's it!" my mom said. "They put an addition on the front. But that's it."

We parked in front of the one-story, ranch-style turquoise

home with a brick walkway. Its front yard was surrounded by a black iron fence with magenta and apricot roses spilling through the spaces. I took pictures, knowing this moment wouldn't present itself again for awhile.

When I was little, my mother told me that once a person dies, their body becomes a shell. "They aren't asleep," she said. "Just gone. I can't explain it. But you know it." This house, too, seemed like a shell without a spirit.

"Your room was right there," my mom said, pointing to the right of the garage, and I turned toward that small piece of real estate, a few hundred square feet on land that could have been the hunting grounds for saber-tooth cats. On the other side of that turquoise paint was the corner where the hamper used to sit, where I set my will in motion and my soul began.

How does the body last? How am I the same package of cells that crawled inside a wicker basket in 1974 and now reclines on a couch 2,000 miles away?

Several years ago, a friend of mine died of cancer at the age of 41. At the viewing, I stood before his body. *My life wouldn't have been the same without you*, I thought, *but now that I'm looking at this sweatered casing, I have to take my memory's word for it.*

As I sat in front of that Maybank house, I had to believe that I'd crawled on the floor as my parents fought, my teenaged sister dated the man she'd still be married to now, and the social order (read "all-white school system") crumbled around them.

A year after my visit to the house, I look up the pictures in my photo cloud and zoom in on the address painted on the curb. 4745 Maybank, as sharp and certain as the gold and lavender gazania daisies packed into a flowerbed asserting their suburban quaintness. I imagine myself into existence, the illusion of history. I place myself in the corner bedroom, tall enough to reach the window. Peering out at three women sitting in a rental car, one of them taking pictures with her phone, I wonder what she thinks she's doing.

~

The country's first walled town, Rossmoor, was an Orange County fortress tucked even further away from the encroaching Other than our Lakewood home had been. It is not a gated subdivision, but an actual unincorporated town of 3,500 tract homes and three elementary schools surrounded by a brick wall. Ross Cortese, son of poor Italian immigrants, envisioned an exclusive community of beautiful, tree-lined neighborhoods. He bought land from Los Alamitos's Fred Bixby Ranch Company to populate with houses priced between $17,000 and $20,000. Earl Kaltenbach, designer of Disneyland's Tomorrowland, was hired to design ranch homes that ended up looking Fantasylandlike, with Rossmoor's signature gingerbread trim and cut-out bird nests under the eaves. If Lakewood was the American Dream, Rossmoor was the American Epiphany.

As a kid, I didn't understand the American or Californian Dream, and I had never heard of the concept of "privilege." I grew up hearing that *we* were the ones who didn't belong, that my friends' families had much more money and that "when you come right down to it, we're poor." My mother would remind me in a hushed voice that my dad's job as a technician at McDonnell Douglas aircraft didn't pay that much. She did not even allow me to say I lived in Rossmoor. I had to write Los Alamitos, the town whose zip code we shared, as my address. This was not about mail delivery; writing "Rossmoor" meant you were a snob. We lived there surreptitiously, by some great accident, and I shouldn't get too comfortable.

But Rossmoor is where I grew up. Orange County, California. White. And white collar. Inside the brick wall. Maybe we didn't drive a Mercedes or take trips to Hawaii, but I always had violin lessons and track shoes, including the fancy racing pair I wore to the big meets. Sports camps or orchestra trips were never a problem. My mom says those extras were affordable only because of her low-wage job in an interior decorating store. Sacrifices made on the brink. "We don't have as much as the others," she'd say, writing out a check for a Scholastic book order, purple-dyed prom shoes, or varsity jacket. We had no credit cards or other debt aside from the mortgage (which my mother often paid ahead). Even when my father went on strike, we had comfortable Christmases. And no matter what the financial or emotional mood in the home, I was always surrounded by decorative beauty.

"But I hate antiques," I would tell my mother while padding across oriental rugs in a house darkened by cabinets of carnival glass and cloisonné. I wanted to live in a house with minimal, modern, black lacquer furniture and Rene Gruau prints. But my mother kept accumulating Victorian-era spoons and commemorative Christmas plates patterned with tastefully whimsical cats.

She was a curator with an endless supply of high-end items gathered at predawn estate sales. Crowded, attractive, and orderly. Even today, with no spaces left on the shelves and walls, my octogenarian mother builds stock off fanciful garden decor: a patch of copper whirligigs among the crepe myrtles, concrete tortoises creeping around the succulents, a ceramic Mediterranean pot that could house a small family.

I have no attachment to things, I tell my husband and kids with an almost buddha-like stoicism. When my wedding ring broke, I ordered another off ebay for $250–a lot cheaper than repairs. I allowed my kids to read and destroy the Dr. Seuss books my mother had saved from my childhood. They sat in a box in her garage for years before she handed them to me to drive back across country in my minivan. What's the point of holding onto a 1976 edition of *The Cat in the Hat?* Will I really take it out of the box and run my fingers over the pages, remembering? My children would inherit them, then their children, handing boxes through the generations, the weight of memory. That's why I let my kids read them until the bindings broke. After my youngest graduated to chapter books, I tossed the Dr. Seuss, relieved.

Several years ago, at the Glen Workshop in Santa Fe, I attended a humanities course taught by author and film critic Jeffrey Overstreet. Along with reading poetry and listening to music, we screened two movies: *Munyurangabo* and *The Summer Hours*. After watching the first, a drama about post-genocide Rwanda filmed on location, I had no desire to watch a movie about upper class French people. How could these characters' "challenges" even qualify as such?

But then I watched it.

Directed by Olivier Assayas and starring Juliette Binoche, Charles Berling, and Jérémie Renier, *The Summer Hours* follows two brothers and a sister dealing with their mother's estate after her death: the house and the many art pieces contained within. Faced with the demands of modern life—family, career, and changing addresses—the siblings face the truth: their childhood home no longer has a purpose. The historical valuables don't go with anything: decor, lifestyle, or an era of teenagers living for the digital moment.

I cried through most of the showing. I wanted the movie to run backward and disappear. I had three young kids at home and simply could not abide the inevitable upheaval of my mom passing. I knew that day was coming, but I had chosen to ignore it until forced to watch these faces tortured with decision and loss. How would I process, both physically and emotionally, so many thousands of items with a sister across the country? How could a house that has been in our family since 1974 be handed off to someone else?

"Strange for the house to be sold, with new routines, other people in it," the youngest brother Jeremie tells his wife. But to me, the idea is more than strange. It is frightening, an invasion of space and memory that leaves me feeling guilty for ever leaving California in the first place. I had started to hide my mother's objects in the crawlspace of my brain a quarter of a century ago when I moved to the Midwest, and now, I was starting to envision them on the counter spaces of a French home in a movie: small embroidered purses, ceramic thimbles, vintage metal advertisements for navel oranges.

What does one do with a passion for objects? Words and music can be tucked into computers and clouds, one phone holding access to the most cherished sounds and turns of phrase. But items are their own thing; the shapes, light, shadow, texture can't be captured by a photograph. And even the "real thing" eventually loses its realness. When I first saw Seurat's "A Sunday Afternoon on the Island of La Grande Jatte" in the Chicago Art Institute, years after studying the image as a fourth-grader, the painting seemed a representation of my memory rather than the other way around. All the touchable things of the world are what connect us to history, of course, outliving generations. And those things must be restored, valued, protected. Contended with.

Eventually, Helene's items get sorted through, some dispersed to her children, some displayed at the Musee d'Orsay. Near the end of the film, we see one of her tables in a gallery, where people walk by and ignore it. As the room empties, the camera stays on the table, leaving us alone with it. The table is tragic precisely because it isn't tragic to anyone else. Even the family will move on, forgetting. That is the way of every object: the moment of creation, the provenance of passion and light that once filled an artist's hours and days with sketching, carving, or blowing, dies while the materials shine, mellow, decay, endure.

At the end of the movie, Helene's teenage grandchildren and their friends throw a party in the mostly-empty house before it goes on the market. It's the last hurrah, tinged with melancholy. For a moment, Sylvie recalls picking cherries with her grandmother. She tells her boyfriend about it, cries briefly, then heads down to the lake to swim.

Rossmoor: the getaway, the fake neighborhood, the down payment on a dream. It's a nice town with high-end real estate and manicured tropical yards, but it doesn't hold the charm of multiple generations on country acreage with French picnic baskets. You can see the 605 freeway from my mother's front yard.

Only 15-20% of Rossmoor houses are "originals"—structures unchanged from their construction in the 1950s. The land is what's valuable. People knock down the gingerbread cottages to build Mediterranean villas with no yards between them. I don't want our family's house to suffer that transformation.

Sometimes I imagine the Newport-Inglewood fault, which runs through the area, taking out the house and my mother with it so she doesn't have to suffer. She and her cat will be watching Downton Abbey when a ram-shaped terracotta pot from Tijuana will come sliding off a high shelf and hit them both in the head. They'll already be knocked out when the whole house comes down. It will be no one's fault but God's, and we can throw our hands up and say, "at least she didn't feel it." And if a year later someone builds a Gatsby-esque mansion atop it, so be it. As long as I don't have to decide.

I won't want to see my mother's items go, but I know I can't take them, either. I don't want to turn my house in the Midwest into the house of my childhood, hauling antiques across the desert, Rockies, and plains. Even my sister, who lives in California in a bigger house, acknowledges that she doesn't have the capacity.

Watching *The Summer Hours* released the grief of knowing we would go through these items and get rid of most of them. We have made our own lives. We do our own thing. We move on. For weeks, months, most likely the better part of a year, a carved jade figurine will make me weep. We will turn it over to other hands and cry over iced tea, and later we will have forgotten it exists.

Subdivisions and walled communities are built on the myth of security, safety from the Other who threatens our comfort and tastes. But the truly dangerous Other is time, the disappearance of generations—the ones who bought the new houses in their heels and coiffed hair mostly dead or in wheelchairs where peace and war, rich and poor, black and white, are in a blur. They remember something that catches their eye, but they can't pass it on to others, a copper whirligig turning, turning in the darkening gallery of their mind.

~

Like the LA River, the San Gabriel River near my home was surrounded by concrete, and I found nothing unusual about that. In fact, I never even realized it was an honest-to-goodness river. It was a suburban bike path about fifty feet above channelized water. I knew nothing of watersheds and the earth's work or this once-wild, winding body of water. My surroundings were designed to fit around me and my life, as was most of suburban Southern California. *We* were the place, earthquakes and water the interruption.

The river bed became famous to me years before I was old enough to ride my bike to the beach. When I was about ten, a helicopter crashed near the entrance to the bike path by the freeway. I was home alone when I heard a labored whirring sound and ran out to the backyard to look at the sky. The helicopter, small and clumsy as a dragonfly, tipped and spun. Just as I began to register that there was something very wrong with this flight, it dropped from sight, and the sky flashed.

"A lot of people died when the sky lit up," my dad said when he got home from work. He was matter-of-fact in a way that made me feel both giddy and nauseated. Something that dramatic could happen near our house? And I saw it happen? It turns out that all six people on board walked away from the crash. The rotor had separated from the rest of the craft, causing the slow spin and sudden plunge through the power lines. Sputter, fall, flash, and live. The river was a place of danger and miracles.

When I moved to the Midwest and started spending time on real rivers—camping, hiking, canoeing—I discovered their innate magic. You sit on the water, and it takes you somewhere else. You find shadowy fish and watch branches wend their way under bridges. You walk a ragged shore. A rural midwestern river is not like the LA or San Gabriel River, molded and managed by engineers. But the San Gabriel gave me the life I needed when I needed it with its smooth, predictable concrete slopes.

As a teenager, before I got my license, I took to escaping to the riverbed on weekends and summer days. One straight shot took me all the way to the beach. Of course, I didn't consider the habit of rivers flowing into oceans. I just knew the river path was a way to get down there without a car, without even stopping for any signals as I flew through Rossmoor and hung a left on the sidewalk by Katella Avenue, picking up the bike bath by the 605 offramp where the helicopter had met its fate.

I eventually stopped wearing a helmet because there were no cars, just a wide berth of concrete and an occasional fellow biker in padded shorts passing me up. I enjoyed the wind in my hair as my skin radiated the pink-brown tint of someone who doesn't really tan. To me, this was as wild as I could get in the guise of safety. No rough edges, just a swift route to the water where I could lay out a beach towel, eat grapes, skim classics, and sense myself approaching the outer edges of greatness.

One afternoon, just as I was starting to pick up the pace in a high gear that made my spokes hum, my backpack swaying from side to side, I heard a bell.

I turned my head quickly. There was my dad, who hadn't been on a bike in years, swaying his way down the path. It didn't take long for me to figure it out: he was coming to ride with me. He was all angles and green metallic 1960s bike, and he was ringing his bell and smiling.

I felt trapped, like a spider suddenly clapped under a cup. For once, I had found a way out of the house and he was treading on that way quite literally, uninvited. I didn't want to accept this bold attempt at father-daughter connection. I wanted him to be *normal*—not barricading my mom and me in our rooms while he watched porn in the living room with a pillow in his lap, not silently standing in the bathroom window to watch my boyfriend and me kiss on the porch or saying bizarre things when my friends were over, like asking Shelly mid-bite if she would just go ahead and give him her fried rice. He just couldn't make up for his trespasses by riding his bike out to meet me unannounced.

I turned around on the path, dragging my feet as I repositioned the bike, and rode toward him. What was I supposed to do? I certainly hoped he hadn't expected to join me at the beach, where after my alone time I planned to meet a friend at the pizza stand.

He called out, "Hey, Tania Bird!" still some distance away. Then his front wheel skidded under him and he fell. I gasped but then remembered that people fell on their bikes all the time and this was nothing to gasp about. I wanted him to spring back up and ride, not because I was worried about him, but because I wanted to say hello, maybe ride with him toward home, then come back by myself. But he stayed down, bike parts and limbs heaped and quiet like a daddy long legs that has drowned in the tub but stopped short of slipping down the drain.

I don't remember what he said, and I don't remember what I said. In fact, I don't know if I ever reached him. I just know that he rode back home, shaken, and I headed back down to the beach. The helicopter crash felt like it made more sense than what had happened that afternoon.

There was a cast the next day, and the overwhelming sense that I had done something wrong. He didn't blame me for the fall, but I felt guilty for the sacrifice he made, for his repeated lament that he just couldn't believe that he didn't remember how to ride a bike, that it was too much, too big of a ride, too soon.

"I shouldn't have done it. It was stupid of me."

Stupid to ride the bike at all? Stupid to come out and try to connect with me? I said nothing. For six weeks I pretended not to see the cast as I grabbed my beach bag and rode off to the sea.

I think about the river, which I now know has been molded and formed to hold the pressure not only of rain, but of people. They burst and press against one another, in an area where it is so hard to get open space. The concrete can't stop the separation of rotor from plane, the separation of father from daughter. There are crashes and then the walking away, the bleeding, and the shaky ride back.

~

I didn't spend enough time with Oscar the tortoise this summer. For forty years I've believed time will never run out.

Visiting California, I took my annual walk through my childhood backyard of bougainvillea, crepe myrtle, and fruit. I picked strawberries, paid homage to my name scratched in a concrete border in 1980, then wandered to the side yard to find Oscar.

I sat in the gravel as he gummed a piece of lettuce hanging in seaweedy strips. He's always been a sloppy eater, clomping around the yard with leftover pollen or hibiscus petals sticking to his mouth. We exchanged eye contact briefly. I tapped his nose, just as I did as an annoying kid, and he snorted, yanking his head back in his shell.

My mother rescued the brooding desert tortoise when I was four. She found him lumbering across the street, a reptilian tank with no regard for traffic. She grabbed the huffing beast and went door to door asking if he belonged to anyone. According to Mom lore, everyone laughed, exclaiming, "We don't want that ugly tortoise!" and slammed the door.

So we took him home. We already owned Choo-Choo, another rescue tortoise my mom acquired when my sister was a baby. Choo-Choo had been found slowly suffocating, as someone had painted her shell red, white, and blue without understanding that tortoises use their shells to breathe. My mom and grandmother spent days peeling the paint off with their fingernails.

Unlike the docile Choo-Choo, Oscar was aggressive.

"He was an angry tortoise back then," Mom told me. "He had a past."

A tortoise specialist told Mom that when Oscar snapped, all she had to do was say "no" and flick his shell. Sure enough, he stopped biting and responded confidently to a life of discipline, lettuce, and love.

I spent a lot of time alone as a child, and the tortoises served as my stalwart playmates. I invited them on my imaginary backyard cruise ship, delivering petal salads arranged in rainbow-order gradations. I carried the tortoises under my arm like library books. And when they mated, a crashing, snuffling affair that never resulted in hatchlings, I politely hula-hooped on the patio until they completed the task.

In the winter, they hibernated. Mom would wrap them in old blankets, tuck them in cardboard boxes, and place the boxes on a shelf in the garage. Come March or so, we'd open the boxes outside and let the tortoises resurrect themselves when they saw fit.

One winter, after I'd been out of the house for years, it warmed up unseasonably early. Oscar crawled out of his garage box, fell off the shelf, and broke his shell. Mom wrapped him in gauze and rocked him through the night.

"He was crying," she said. "Both of us were."

Choo-Choo died a few years ago at the younger end of the tortoise lifespan of eighty to one hundred years. Oscar is around fifty or sixty to my forty-something, putting us neck and neck. But I want him to lose this race toward death.

Oscar has to outlive me, for as soon as he dies, history will take a serious turn. When I visit the backyard, he is there, munching on my mom's organic offerings. My mom is still there, yes, but her stature continues to shrink and her skin continues to sag. She speaks casually of her mini-strokes.

The household antiques imprinted in my memory may stay in the family for hundreds of years, but they don't have a pulse. Oscar is a living artifact, my one breathing, unchanging connection to the afternoons I spent telling stories to the soundtrack of doves, coastal winds, and the 605 freeway, whose sustained hum still comforts me.

"Do you think he recognized me?" I asked my mom this summer. Like a child asking about Santa, I knew the answer but wanted her to say, *yes,* that even though I've been away from home since 1990, my face and voice are somehow locked inside his scaly head.

"Tortoises are very intelligent," she replied right away. "I just got new stepping stones, and Oscar immediately came over to check them out."

"Have you made…plans for him? You know, in case you…"

"Well, no. I guess not."

I was glad to hear it.

The famous philosopher Steven Wright once said, "I intend to live forever. So far, so good." No matter the billions of mortal examples set before us, most of us believe on a visceral level there will always be a place to return to: a house, parent, landscape, tortoise.

Of course I want to live a long time. But I want Oscar to

live even longer. I want him to die after all of us are gone, slipping out of consciousness to the memory of my eyes, the wind blowing through the hibiscus flowers, my mom cooing, "Let's keep him. He's a tortoise worth holding onto."

BEACH BOYS

"I love the beach, but the beach hates me," was my mother's mantra. And with that, I rarely visited the Pacific Ocean that roared and crashed just five miles from my house.

The sun will kill you, she insisted. It will burn you and suck you dry. You will get spots and cancer and the salt water will sting your eyes, and the sand will never get out of the rug.

My mother was a redhead with blue eyes. She wore large straw hats when she gardened, and as far as I knew, did not own a swimsuit. Solutions like beach umbrellas, sunscreen, and long-sleeved cover-ups were available, but once she made up her mind, she couldn't unmake it. She was not a beach person.

My friend Shelly lived in neighboring Seal Beach on Third Street, just a few blocks from the ocean and accessible by the river channel bike path. Her house was magic. A stained-glass window liquified the sun to blue streams on the living room floor. Her stepmother kept a steady supply of seashells in glass bowls and yogurt topped with granola and fresh fruit.

A mother and baby dolphin, painted by a local muralist, swam across Shelly's bedroom wall. On long afternoons we listened to "Life In a Northern Town" by the Dream Academy, waves whooshing in the pauses between repeats. We weren't in England nor the north, but the song caught our breath.

I was mere miles from my Rossmoor doorstep but at the literal end of the continent. In a decade we'd be at the end of the millennium and already felt that cosmic pressure, answering essay prompts like, "Where do you see yourself in the year 2000?" Like the waves themselves, the future washed over my feet with relief and anxiety. Cool, glistening, and full of hidden kelp that tangled my feet. California waters were dark.

I wasn't a popular girl in high school. Awkward and artsy, I managed to escape being asked to any dances save my disastrous senior prom. But in my bathing suit, I was a tall and willowy clean slate with mile-long legs and breasts like half-oranges: not huge but cheerfully proportioned. When I put on a bathing suit, I could draw the attention of men and boys without having to talk to them. Their admiring looks were enough to get me started on my long, tedious education on the uneasy power of male-female dynamics.

The first swimsuit I bought was a white, black, and silver speckled bikini. I had never been good at putting together outfits and hated buying shoes for my size-10 feet. But with one hook of a strapless top, I looked good. The silver squares caught the light, and I wore that light with pride.

Soon I discovered that by visiting the department store clearance rack, I could gather up a number of bronze and snake-skin bikinis, teal bandeaus, and strappy cherry-printed numbers with ties brushing my thighs. As I walked the sands of Seal Beach, Sunset, and Huntington, I learned that seven dollars of fabric could wield tremendous power.

I'm light skinned and burn easily, but I started to train myself into getting tan, gradually lowering the SPF number as the season progressed. When I reached SPF four and took on the sheen of a roasted marshmallow, I felt I had accomplished something, a teenage OC girl rite of passage.

To prepare for my beach days, I took to laying out in my own backyard on the chaise lounge in my original metallic bikini. I listened to music on my Walkman cassette player as our pet desert tortoises crept across the lawn chewing on fallen hibiscus petals. The occasional crepe myrtle petal flew into my hair.

One day I sensed a presence. It was my father at the window, inside the house, holding a camera. He'd been snapping pictures.

"What are you doing?" I asked through the screen.

"Just curious," he said. "I wanted to see how you were put together."

I said nothing. Shame prickled my body, and my stomach sank in the same way it did when I discovered the old Playboy magazines in his dresser years before. When I first found them, I was thrilled, then scared, then numbed by the doe-eyed nude blondes I'd visit occasionally out of a sense of somber duty. I was a woman now, not even immune to the gaze of my own father. The terror of my body had arrived. It had been seen, scrutinized, and recorded on a film negative that would later be developed and placed before me on the kitchen counter. On that 4x6 glossy rectangle, my metallic speckled suit appeared suddenly ridiculous against the forced-caramel skin of my stomach and slightly pink tinge of my thighs. Something about my breasts and hair seemed tired, stuck on. I was a mousily sluggish centerfold.

I never sunbathed at my house again.

From that point forward, I didn't want my father to notice me at all. Even on the night of the prom, the evening everyone stands in their front yards with their parents taking pictures, I hid in the bathroom fussing with my fifty-color eyeshadow set. I didn't want him to see me with my smokey plum eyes and teased hair. I was just short of eighteen, almost the age of the women in the magazines at the bottom of his dresser drawer.

I wore a black sequined, royal purple dress with a black bow at the waist and shoes I had dyed purple. When my date and our friends arrived in a borrowed Mercedes, I rushed down the driveway to spend the evening with a boy I would later find out wished he'd taken someone else.

For years, I did not want my father to hug me, and when he did, I made sure the embrace was shallow and quick. I was afraid of my breasts making contact with his body, and even on my wedding day I did not make eye contact with him as he readied to walk me down the aisle.

I feared my beauty while nurturing it. I wanted to hide from men while also pleasing them. Perhaps the fact that I didn't know how to talk to them saved me from seeking their attention in a promiscuous manner. I attended a college with coed dorms and never laid a finger on a man nor encouraged one to enter my room. But I walked the hallway smiling at everyone, wearing sweet floral sundresses without bras.

One male dorm mate asked me what the deal was with that. "Because the straps poke out," I said. "No one's looking, anyway." I didn't think I was lying. The dress in question was a long ivory silky A-line with orange, teal, and hot pink paisleys and a thick sash at the waist. A bra got in the way of the flow, so I opted out. I was not large-breasted, flirtatious, nor sexy. I was away from home for the first time, safe.

"No one's looking?" he muttered. "Uh huh." I crossed my

arms and looked down. I felt ashamed of my body but also of my innocence, which betrayed my ignorance of the male mind. Did all men have dark thoughts about women? Or was it just my father? I wanted to start a new life with men but found myself being used in spite of myself.

My freshman year I developed a crush on a dark-haired senior, Tom, who lived directly across the hall. He had a girlfriend in England whom he often fought with on the phone late at night after drinking. There was not much to see in him aside from his dark hair that hung over his eyes, his deep voice, and the fact that he held an editorial position at the university paper. Mostly, he was close by and willing to interact with me without much effort on my part.

One night he charged into my room, angry with his girlfriend. He yanked my miniature Christmas tree from my shelf and hurled it across my room, ornaments shattering. He stormed back out, and I cleaned up the mess without a word.

Another time he sauntered over to my room to gaze at my Picasso print of "The Three Musicians" longingly.

"That would sure look good in my newspaper office," he sighed.

I let him borrow the poster. As the school year neared its end, I asked him to return it. "Sure, tomorrow," he'd say. He said it every time I asked.

On move-out day, I reminded him once more. "Going to the office now," he said, and disappeared. I waited there in my empty room, car packed. Of course Tom never returned. As I drove the freeway back home, the first summer after my father left my mother, I hated myself. The sun blasted through the car window onto my bare thighs. Despite the heat, I wanted to cover up.

A few years back, for the first time in my adult life, I visited California on my own, landing on an LAX runway bordered with wild orange poppies. I attended a writing conference in Los Angeles while bouncing from relative to relative and reprocessing my traumatic associations with freeways, fault lines, and memory. On a bit of a whim the last afternoon of my visit, I asked my mom if she and her longtime best friend Gary wanted to accompany me to Seal Beach. No swimsuits or water: just walking along the pier.

"Oh, I don't know," my mom said, her once-red hair framing her face in a ring of wisps escaping from a bun. "The parking has just gotten so expensive. Only the rich can go down there these days," she said.

"Don't worry," I said. "It will be my treat."

My mother and Gary and I took the ten-minute drive and paid three dollars for parking. My mother couldn't believe it, thinking for decades that not only was the beach dangerous, but cost-prohibitive. She looked around in wonder as seagulls swooped around the electric wires and waves beat against the barnacled pier.

"This is so fun!" she exclaimed. She was eighty and visiting the charming beach in her own backyard for the first time in perhaps twenty, thirty years. Maybe longer. Gary, a slight man in thick glasses and a cardigan, eight years my mother's junior, quietly walked alongside us with occasional remarks about the history of Seal Beach and its Naval Weapons station.

We strolled to the end of Seal Beach Pier, the site of a few ill-fated high school dates, and, eventually, long walks with my husband-to-be, who would propose at water's edge. Middle aged men, most of them Hispanic and some of them playing soft music through portable radios, fished off the pier with buckets at their feet. Sadly, the once iconic Ruby's Diner at the end of the pier was gone, replaced with a chain-link fence and building ruins. When we got to the fence, we turned around and walked back. The sun had started to sink to the west, which was not, amazingly, the ocean. Seal Beach faced south.

"I should do this again," my mom said. "Gary, shouldn't we do this again?" He nodded, scratched his gray beard, and gazed out at the water.

I offered to buy them coffee at a shop I didn't recognize. To my mother, this was another major purchase, but she assented—plain coffee, black. Fancy drinks were out of the question.

We sat on a bench on Main Street. My mother wore an oversized white T-shirt printed with puppies and kittens: a gift from the Humane Society, a place that receives her constant donations. Like my mother, I wore my hair in a bun, wispy tendrils flying in the seaside breeze. Ever since turning forty, I've felt a little more attractive, happy with my tall stature and the way my glasses rest on the high cheekbones I used to think made me look like a child with a scrunched up smile and big nose. I've gained weight around my middle but now look people solidly in the eyes. I allowed the cappuccino to wash over me, the fears I'd held in my body for so many years escaping like steam through the lid's tiny window.

Now the power of my body is in the deciding. Deciding to fill it with good things and sweet things, adorning it with scarves the color of beach sunsets. Driving my body to an airport, putting my body on a plane and a car and bringing it into the rooms of people I love and people I decide to forgive.

Across the street, the ice cream and candy shop from my childhood, Grandma's, is gone, replaced with a Cold Stone Creamery. Businesses change with the generations, and although it's sad when families hit hard financial times, I've never understood the almost angry nostalgia with which people regard new establishments. This new shop will be as important to the class of 2025 as the other was to the class of 1990. The lives that are the center of the universe spin on, memories made and memoirs written in these repurposed spaces.

A teenaged girl walks out with a cardboard cup of ice cream. It's too cold for bathing suits, but she works at what a SoCal girl on the beach is expected to do: look beautiful. She wears frayed shorts and a beige shawl-like sweater and short UGG boots. Streaks of green-dyed hair, a mainstream look, twist into her elaborate ponytail. I'm almost the age my mother was when I began to spend hours at the beach seeking validation in my body while trying to escape it. I have a teenage daughter now whom I'm trying to teach to love her body.

The girl crosses the street toward us, her shawl caught up by licks of wind. She's alone but will most likely later meet up with friends who've veered off to other snack shops. She turns the pink spoon upside down and scrapes off her ice cream with her teeth, something I learned to do when I was young so I wouldn't smear my lip gloss.

"That's a pretty girl," my mom says, and I nod.

The sun drops even more, gold brushing our eyelids. I place my hand on my mom's shoulder as she wraps her hands around the cup and gulls screech at the waves. I doubt she'll return until I visit California again. But today we're here, enjoying life in a southern town, sipping and breathing. Today, the beach loves us.

~

The first church I attended as a teenaged new believer swiftly taught me two doctrines: 1) There won't be any Democrats in heaven and 2) Secular music is tantamount to heresy.

The first one was easy enough to get. Reagan had saved us from the devil Jimmy Carter, and now Jesus had the go-ahead to return whenever he wanted. The second proved a little more complicated. What was I supposed to listen to?

The youth pastor's wife took me to a Christian book store so I could tell the musically-redeemed clerk about my favorite bands and find equivalencies worthy of the kingdom of God. My ears turned pink as I told the 20-something, crisp-collared man about the Beatles, Erasure, and Siouxsie and the Banshees cassettes rattling around in my passenger seat. He raised his eyebrows, then grabbed a copy of *Maranatha Praise,* Volume 6, the closest match. I put it in my tape deck on the way to school the next morning, a first step to my journey of spiritual transformation.

It wasn't long, however, before I learned that church leadership made an exception to the ban on secular music. One afternoon, at our Baptist picnic overflowing with potato and Jell-O salads, I heard the familiar references to waves and bushy-bushy blond hairdos whining from the portable radio.

"Why do they have that music on?" I asked my friend Liz.

She smirked. "The Beach Boys are always okay."

"Why?"

She shrugged. "Maybe because they're local. Maybe because they're wholesome. Yeah, right. Like what do they think those 'good vibrations' are really about?"

I laughed with her. I had no idea about the answer.

The Beach Boys swept the world in the 1960s. The Wilson brothers, cousin Alan Jardine, and friend Mike Love grew up in Hawthorne, California, just twenty miles from my hometown. Our close family friend, Gary, attended high school and played football with them, somehow causing Al to break his leg during a bad play. I grew up hearing my dad play The Beach Boys' greatest hits on LP on a weekly basis.

And they really got on my nerves.

The Boys' bright harmonies didn't conjure up fun afternoons of splashing on the beach. They induced head pain, like a glare on the windshield. Even as a little girl I felt put off by "California Girls," that song that categorized women's sex appeal by time zones. When my dad turned up the refrigerator-sized speakers and sang along, I felt vaguely ashamed for being a girl, particularly a California girl who had to live up to the expectations placed upon "the cutest girls in the world." The pressure was real. As one boy said of me in high school, "She's pretty enough. But she's not rad." He might as well have said I was a troll.

Eventually I went back to my Beatles and for the next two and a half decades, any mention of The Beach Boys set my eyes rolling as I remembered those boppy, cringe-worthy choruses.

Recently, I had the idea to start writing a book about Appalachian fiddle music. Having spent the past several years working on Irish, Scottish, and then old time tunes, I was fascinated with the deep history and heritage of the music. But I felt like an imposter, with no roots in Appalachia or Scotland.

"I grew up in the southern California suburbs. What kind of music IS my music?" I joked with a musically-inclined poet-friend. "The Beach Boys?"

"Maybe," he said. "Listen to their album *Pet Sounds*. Many consider it groundbreaking. Maybe you can learn one of those songs on your fiddle."

I had never heard of *Pet Sounds*—no specific Beach Boys albums, in fact, beyond the "greatest hits" compilations—and had a hard time believing anything by them was "groundbreaking" or worthy of artistic analysis. I continued along with my tunes, listening to "Wayfaring Stranger" and "Shady Grove," jealous of generations of coal miners and butter churners who had real stories to tell.

But finally, I looked up *Pet Sounds*. I listened on repeat and soon found myself singing about Caroline and Sloop John and heads on shoulders, my surprised heart weaving in and out of flutes, sleigh bells, bassoons, and dogs.

The movie *Love and Mercy* (2014) follows Brian Wilson's fragile state of mind while producing *Pet Sounds*, an album few people believed in, as it strayed from the Beach Boys's usual surf-rock fare. I learned that Brian Wilson is a real, suffering, vulnerable human being. He wasn't a carefree surfer. (None of them ever were, except for Dennis, the most "California" of the group). He heard voices. He fought for his father's approval. He turned to drugs. In later life, he struggled at the hands of his abusive therapist, Ed Landy.

I was almost in tears. Why was I surprised to learn of the

extent of this man's rich inner life? Why was I surprised to realize that the surf music, while fun and catchy and influential in its own right, was a veneer for Wilson's uneasy cocktail of brilliance and mental illness?

I, too, rarely felt at home on the beach. I couldn't swim until I was a teenager. I hated the sand between my toes and the murky mix of mussels and kelp. Anxiety kept me from living the life of a carefree California girl.

The most powerful moment of the movie is when one of the production guys talks to Brian outside the studio after a challenging recording session. "You've gotta know that you're touched, kid," he says. "You've blown our minds." Brian breaks into a smile that seems to emanate from some long-lost golden cells in his body. He is finally seen for who he is, and for one perfect moment can rest in that truth.

After *Pet Sounds*, Brian would work on an even more unusual album, *SMiLE*. "It fell apart for so many reasons. It fell apart for every reason," Wilson writes in his autobiography, *I am Brian Wilson*. He would finally release the *SMiLE Sessions* in 2011, writing that "In my sixties I did what I couldn't do in my twenties."

Musically speaking, he had what it took in his twenties. But navigating stress and mental illness, difficulty with his song partner, Mike Love, and the presence of drugs like LSD would stall the ambitious project. More than anything, the pressure of being a musical commodity got in the way of Wilson's art. According to David Beard of *Goldmine* magazine, Wilson's "…emotions were continuously stifled by the demands placed on him to provide new material that was relatable to the more accessible sun-soaked imagery of the group's moniker. This became problematic for Wilson, because he was far more interested in the compositional connection between how he felt and the best way to communicate his feelings utilizing chord progressions."

It's a romantic notion, the artist trying to break through commercial expectations with his artistic emotions. But it wreaked havoc on the brilliant and sensitive Wilson who labored near the ocean without swimming or surfing, ripping through his own swirling barrel of his mind.

Like Brian, I have fought to stay myself, even when my writing and body have seemingly fallen short. When I've let others down. It can take a lot of work, a lot of false starts, to realize the work has already been done. You're already *you,* and you just need to find it.

California's "aggressively relaxed attitude," which William Finnegan describes in his surfing memoir *Barbarian Days: A Surfing Life,* intimidated me for the first twenty-one years of my life. I still dread it whenever I visit. The expectation to remain happy and calm is itself a source of stress. Images of the SoCal good life—bikes weaving around the boardwalk, blue water and shadows mingling with underwater pool lights, hair flying in the wind of a high-speed Pacific Coast Highway—put me on edge. *You live where everyone else wants to live, with the sunny wonder of an orange crate label. Don't complain. Don't hide from the sun. Get out and enjoy life.*

But what if you can't? What if "getting around," to you, is driving up and down the same old strip of your mind?

On a rainy October night, I went to see Brian Wilson perform at the Rosemont Theatre outside of Chicago. I wasn't the only one to show up in a Hawaiian shirt, which rippled like a flag in the humid breeze. In my mid-40s, I was among the younger people in the venue, but I was relieved it was a sit-down concert without an opener. An 8pm start time was already pushing it.

The band, around a dozen members that included Alan Jardine and his son Matthew, would came out to take their places on the stage, Brian Wilson among them without any special introduction or fanfare. He walked in a strange way, a bit hunched with a hobbling, but speedy gait, a bandmate at his elbow to steady him. He sat down immediately, as matter-of-factly as he were taking his place at a workbench.

They would open with "California Girls," and I found myself singing to the song I had always hated. I felt a bit of pride for being a native, a sense of reckless comfort in myself, and belted out the songs with my friend by my side, dancing in our seats. Then "Dance, Dance, Dance," "Little Deuce Coupe." He slowed down with "In My Room," which I surreptitiously taped live for Facebook so my California friend recovering from a suicide attempt could watch.

The truth is that Brian Wilson's voice is failing. Whether because of cigarettes, drugs, age, or the physical exhaustion that comes from mental illness, his once liquid falsetto is now gravelly, and he seems to speak rather than sing. But when you see him, you don't care. During the second half of the concert, when the band would perform *Pet Sounds* from beginning to end, Brian would sing "God Only Knows," and we would fall silent, stunned into history. He spoke the song rather than sang it, the frailty of this aging survivor making the song all the more beautiful.

Since then, I have pulled out my fiddle and sounded out

"God Only Knows." When I play it myself, the tune suddenly becomes more complicated, but Wilson purifies the emotional and musical complexity into a lush, repeating wave that washes over my skin. This is my "religious music." Not because it is "fun and wholesome" or even because it mentions God, but because this California girl has found some peace in her Midwestern living room while drawing the bow across the strings.

~

The Beach Boys' 1966 promotion video for "Sloop John B" is unsophisticated, repetitive, and completely mesmerizing.

For just shy of three minutes, five grown men frolic in Brian Wilson's backyard pool like clumsy puppies, rolling around on an inflatable raft while their version of the Jamaican folk song provides the soundtrack. The video lacks the quick cuts and special effects of modern music videos, unless you want to describe the beginning, when Brian greets every band member until finally shaking hands with himself, as a special effect.

It's so SoCal, this patio jaunt. Life appears timelessly fun under the persistent rays (the black and white film still scintillates with sunshine), but underneath the concrete floor of the pool are the tremors: every day's handful of literal earthquakes, mostly undetected without sensitive seismographs, and the existential quivers from living in a place fraught with such uneasy beauty. At the time of the filming, the fault lines of mental illness were starting to crack in Brian's brain.

I watch the video over and over, listen to "Sloop John B" on repeat. At first I don't ask why: these days, I indulge my desires to submerge myself in something and psychoanalyze myself, if at all, later. But the message has become unmistakable: The more I listen to one of my favorite "new" songs, which is now over fifty years old, the more I sense I've known it all along.

I read up on the history. Originally a Bahamian folk song known as "The John B. Sails," the tune was first transcribed by Richard Le Gallienne in 1916 and then later published by Carl Sandburg in *The American Songbag* in 1927. I listen to a number of pre-Beach Boys recordings, including renditions by Gerry Butler, Johnny Cash, and the Kingston Trio. And that is where I stop.

The Kingston Trio record that pops up on Spotify, their debut, self-titled album released in 1958 with the three acoustic-guitar-and-banjo-playing fellows on a plain red background, was one of my father's favorites. When my mother worked at the store on Saturdays and I stayed home alone with my dad, we went to my violin lessons, grabbed cheeseburgers at Jack-in-the-Box, then went home, usually orbiting around our separate interests until my mom got home. But sometimes we listened to music together—always his choice of records. These albums became part of my childhood canon, so that when I play Kingston Trio now, it's like the songs never left my head.

They sing about Sloop John, but with a lot more banjo and a lot less vocal range than the Beach Boys. And their plaintive lyrics about wishing to go home cut into the tender patch of skin stretching tautly over my memory. Is it *home* that I'm longing for or *the wanting* itself? Can I be homesick for homesickness, a feeling I never got after leaving the Golden State?

The trio also sings about Tom Dooley. Even though Dooley was a murderer, and the female victim he stabbed had undoubtedly suffered her own agony, the refrain about a poor boy bound to die haunted me. Could there be anything worse than knowing that he'd be hanging from an oak tree by tomorrow?

There was also "Scotch and Soda," breathless and soothing while vaguely unsettling, as alcohol normally meant chaos and anger to me. And "Saro Jane" and "Little Maggie" and the "Three Jolly Coachmen" (with the funny chuckles–Ha-ha-ha! Ho-ho-ho!–I learned to add at the right times), songs I've been drawn to in different renditions over the years without realizing we already had a forty-year history.

Our catalog of maritime music didn't stop with John B's miserable journey. We sailed with the *Pirates of Penzance* and the navy of the *South Pacific*, plumbed the depths of Harry Belafonte's *Mark Twain and Other Folk Favorites,* an album cover I always remembered featuring Belafonte's head on a buoy.

Maine is where the next record, Dad's musical gold standard, took us. *Carousel*, another Rodgers and Hammerstein musical, focuses on gruff Billy Bigelow, a barker who meets Julie, a young millworker visiting the carnival. He marries her and gets promptly fired by Ms. Mullins, his jealous boss. Failing to find another job and suffering under the wounded pride of having to move in with Julie's cousin, Billy takes to hitting his wife and participating in a theft gone wrong that ends with his stabbing himself. And oh yeah: at this point, Julie is pregnant.

At the gates of heaven, Billy is given a chance to rectify past mistakes so he can possibly make the cut for entrance. He returns to earth to try to help his now teenaged, bitter outcast of a daughter, Louise. In the end, he presents a gift of a heavenly star to Louise, sees her through her high school graduation (albeit invisibly) and, having righted himself, returns for his eternal reward.

What is intended as an emotional touchstone of the *Carousel* musical, "Soliloquy," filled me with dread. This is the song my dad would listen to, or, worse, watch on video—Gordon MacRae strolling the Maine shores in his mile-high pants—and sob.

Upon finding out Julie is pregnant, Billy sings a triumphant anthem to his future son, Bill. Then suddenly, as if he has never considered the basic statistics of human reproduction, it hits him: what if his boy is born a girl?

My father didn't outright cry at first, but stared straight ahead, his white hanky poised near his nose. Then he would start to hiccup and gasp. I never knew what to do. Although the song had turned to the subject of fathers and daughters, it seemed a private matter. I was embarrassed by feelings of shame that came from my father's disjointed emotions refracted by songs.

What did it mean to be a daughter? I was lanky and awkward and terrified of everything, but I wasn't looking for paternal protection that the song suggested was the heritage of daughters. If anything, I wanted peace and quiet and structure in my home. I wanted predictable emotions, not yelling about unchanged light bulbs one night and crying the next as we watched a 1950s actor saunter along the Atlantic shore dreaming about a little girl yet to be born. Here I was, already born, and I didn't know what to do with my father's tears.

Today, as I listen to "Sloop John B," I struggle with aligning my feelings. At once lost at sea and yearning for freeze frames of my childhood, the California sun lighting up dust motes in the living room while I sit with my father, I listen because my brain leads my finger to press the play button one more time, and although I don't understand this desire, I need it.

In his autobiography *I am Brian Wilson*, Wilson equivocates on the topic of his father. He doesn't want to write his father off. He makes an effort to recognize his father's talent and contribution to The Beach Boys legacy but wants to recognize the difficulty he has caused—the physical abuse, the belittling comments, the unpredictable loss of temper. He carries his father's memory like a surfboard under his arm that he never carried in real life but in pictures and the nation's consciousness. I carry my father's records and WWII movies and model trains, all the brilliant minutia of a life built by an impassioned, detached curiosity about the world.

Brian Wilson was not entirely happy when he filmed the promo video for Sloop. But he smiled anyway. Much is made about "being real" these days. *Don't smile when you're actually sad.* But you've also got to find a way to survive, to splash around the pool when you feel like you're sinking. Salvation can be found in the power to find a modicum of light. To remember a good memory, or to even *create* a good memory that wasn't there in the first place, reveals the imagination of the soul to hold onto what is true and beautiful and lovely. Smiles that don't make sense can sometimes heal.

The Sloop passenger sings that he wants to go home—the only place that can save him from drunks, thieves, and hunger. But what *is* home for him? It's certainly not the same as family, for the song starts with the speaker fighting with his grandfather, who he wants to escape. I'd like to think the sailor's home is more than just a physical, landward place to sleep, but he doesn't sing much about *that* place either. Home is more the *absence* of where he is now, the *wanting* of peace and stability. Home is in his *will* to be somewhere else.

My home base, too, is in the wanting. Maybe even running straight into memory, emailing my aged father out of the blue one night, despite that he never became what I wanted him to be: *remember when I was a little girl, and we listened to those records over and over?*

STARS

Every Southern Californian has their brush-with-fame stories. It's a rite of passage, that time you ran into John Lithgow in the produce aisle or Rob Lowe at a stoplight. One friend had the pleasure of petting Stephen Spielberg's dog; another found herself browsing a garage sale alongside Frances McDormand. Somehow, my mother ended up on a sailboat with Mel Blanc, the voice of Bugs Bunny, and wrapped gifts for a fundraiser alongside Debbie Reynolds, whose bare feet became a part of our family's mythology.

In the 80s, several of my fellow high school freshmen played extras in the Kirk Cameron/Dudley Moore film, *Like Father Like Son.* Throughout the movie, classroom and hallway scenes look just like those from my high school—not only the puffy bangs and stonewashed jeans, but the actual faces. As Cameron fumbled through presentations, cafeteria mishaps, and lockerside conversations with girls, my real-life peers watched, mouths agape.

I did not participate in the Kirk Cameron movie, but during my sophomore year of college, I was invited by my roommate's cousin to watch Jason Priestley film a scene for *Calendar Girl.* The 1993 movie, which now comes off as downright creepy, follows three high school boys in 1962 going off on one last jaunt before facing the responsibilities of "real life." Their mission is to find Marilyn Monroe and demand her for a date. Nude pictures, heavy innuendo, and stalking Marilyn outside her house for hours at a time are all part of the bonding experience.

The scene I watched took place in the Redlands Fox Theatre, a historic building located a couple towns over from my college. The characters had just finished watching *Some Like it Hot,* ogling their goddess. For a couple of hours, my roommate and I sat in the back, watching Roy Darpinian (Jason Priestley) jump over and around the movie seats as he tried to convince Ned Bleuer (Gabriel Olds) and Scott Foreman (Jerry O'Connell) to come on the road trip to find Marilyn. After the filming, I was introduced to Priestly, whom I towered over awkwardly as I shook his hand, and realized the whole afternoon was rather embarrassing and dull. Why, exactly, did I take time off work to go? But it's a story I tell, and one that I will continue to share, as I come to terms with southern California's proximity to, and distance from, the stars.

Until you appear on camera yourself, you have not truly experienced the flow of Hollywood into your life. When I was in ninth grade, my community youth orchestra was invited to play at the Los Angeles County Holiday Celebration, a daylong concert held at the Dorothy Chandler Pavilion every Christmas Eve since 1960. The whole show is televised live on PBS, the perfect background companion to wrapping presents and preparing dishes on a long, hazy southern California December 24th.

This performance would mark my first time on camera, and I was ready to make a splash. Wearing the same pale pink polyester dress I wore to any dressy event, and plenty of glittery aqua eyeshadow, I walked on stage and found my seat among the sea of violins. I slipped into my folding chair and turned toward the blazing lights.

Watching the VHS tape at home later that night, I sat patiently waiting for my moment. I watched us play the "Dance of the Sugar Plum Fairies," a medley of carols, and "Rudolph the Red-Nosed Reindeer." Finally, during "Sleigh Bells"—da da da DA–the camera zoomed in on my pale face. At that moment, my nose twitched rapidly, apparently from an itch or an intercepted sneeze. The camera then panned over to the sophisticated, non-twitching violists, and that was the end of my fame. I rewound and watched that performance over and over, hoping I would look less like a rabbit each time. But with every playback, I seemed to grow even more ridiculous. I may as well have had whiskers and ears.

That same year, I had decided I wanted to become a screenwriter. I signed up for a class at the park district, the only youngster in a room full of middle-aged people. Our balding teacher in sagging pleated pants so believed in the perfection of *First Blood* as a script, he had us watch the whole thing on the first night. Sensitive to even the mildest movie violence, I averted my eyes for most of the viewing, pretending to write notes in my binder. But when I got home that night, I promptly wrote a scene inspired by my freshman history teacher, a man who punched holes in walls and made kids do push ups when they missed questions during oral quizzes, or "roastings." Like Sylvester Stallone's character of John J. Rambo, Mr. Loftus was misunderstood and capable of the great horror that made me feel famous to be in his class. I tried to rein in his power with the ribbons of my Brother typewriter.

As the story goes, the screenwriting teacher was so impressed with my work, he called my mom and told her he wanted to give me a scholarship to move to Hollywood and begin screenwriting school. I was 14, and she promptly said no. Today, I have no idea what the school was or how they were planning on giving me a complete high school education. Would I spend the days writing and the evenings partying like Drew Barrymore? I wanted to ask questions but was afraid to find out it wasn't actually true.

A couple years later, I found myself tasked with living a less secular life. Christian radio stations advertised conservative art shows and family-friendly books. Trying to integrate faith into my life by surrounding myself with Christian labels, I heard a call for extras to participate in a Focus on the Family movie. I would need to get myself there, then I would enjoy a day of catered lunch and fame as I worked to bring light to the entertainment industry.

I would be needed at a high school in Whittier on a Saturday morning, where I would be fitted for a graduation gown, wait an hour or so, heap a paper plate with mashed potatoes and cold cut sandwiches, and wait an hour more. Finally, I would line up with the other "graduates" in preparation for the big scene: receiving a diploma and shaking a principal's hand.

I could never remember the name of the film, so recently I looked online then contacted Focus on the Family myself. "Although we can't be certain," a representative replied to my request, "we believe the film you're referring to may be either *Molder of Dreams* (1989) or *Teacher of the Year* (1990)." Both movies, which are part classroom reenactment and part motivational speaking, feature Guy Doud as himself, a public high school English teacher from Minnesota who funneled his painful childhood experiences with bullying and rejection into encouraging students toward self-acceptance and excellence. I suspected my movie was *Teacher of the Year* because of the release date—1989 would be too early—and went on a quest to find it.

It wasn't easy. The movie is no longer produced or sold, even by Focus on the Family; neither is it accessible via streaming or YouTube. Library, no dice. Same with ebay. Finally, I contacted a librarian friend who said she might be able to get it through interlibrary loan—not the system within the district network, which showed no sign of *Teacher of the Year,* but the hardcore, last-resort loan system that magically locates dusty, forgotten materials in university basements and weeks later brings you the news that you, strange obsessive person, are now the official temporary guardian of a book or media source that no one has touched in decades.

After picking up the movie, I stopped by my friend's house to borrow a VHS player. This was throwback at an extreme. On the evening I pressed play, none of my children expressed interest. "But I might be in it," I said, and they looked at me blankly.

I set my treadmill to a moderate pace and watched the film unfold until the end, with its reenacted graduation scene, where Guy Doud watches actors portraying some of his students, most poignantly the boy with cancer near the end of his life, receive their diplomas. Before that heart wrenching moment, several students walk across the stage to shake hands with the principal and take their rolled-up papers. At that point, I stopped walking on the treadmill, got off the couch, and walked right up to the screen.

There's a tall figure in line, just a shape lit with golden brown hair who smiles self-consciously before loping to the front. At first I'm not sure if it's me. With so many extras that day, what are the chances I made the cut?

But then the figure rounds a few rows of chairs, shakes hands with the principal, and raises a fist in victory. I hit pause. It's me, walking and gesturing in a way only I can.

Suddenly, I'm back in that gym, holding the diploma, the taste of potato salad still in my mouth. I'm smiling with the excitement of being seen, recorded, contributing to something larger than my insular life by participating in an insular project.

Of course, these three seconds of footage mean nothing. Like the nose twitch at the Dorothy Chandler Pavilion, it's a moment that no one remembers but me. Then why are those moments so distinct in my catalog of images from the past, moments in time captured with a camera now decades buried in a landfill?

Every moment on camera is a fresh opportunity to ignite a spark that fades immediately. Think of all the sitcom episodes and low-rated movies and soap operas rolling like salt water taffy, fluidly magic for a moment then eaten, digested and disposed of as quickly as the echo of *action!* dissipates.

I rewind and pause *Teacher of the Year* again and again, alone in my basement, to the hand shake and raised fist, that quick suspension of the ordinary of seeing myself on screen in a movie that no longer exists. And perhaps that's what the camera does—lifts us from our everyday, unseen lives, replaying us, and for a moment, making us perhaps more immortal.

It's a strange fixation, that if you show up on a screen,

especially in the days before YouTube, you have somehow earned it. Someone has vetted you, a space in time, and justified your place there. Someone has set up a machine and allowed you to take up film or digital space. It's why movie stars always look smaller in real life, and why meeting them is never as exciting as the story about meeting them, or the anticipation of such.

Cintra Wilson, in her book *A Massive Swelling: Celebrity Reexamined as a Grotesque Crippling Disease*, decries the notion of celebrity as some sick, cruel joke on the rest of us, who regard stars as "an untouchable royal family, which causes most of us to act like dribbling serfs despite the value of our individual lives. We regard ourselves as slow-minded, vermin-infested bed-wetters when presented with the gold-plated aura of media success in others." Her writing is downright poetic and entertaining, meant to instruct as well as delight, but there is power in her words. Even after all these years, as a mature, middle-aged, somewhat actualized woman of letters, I need the reminder that I am a celebrity to my family and friends, that we are royalty to each other, and that is what matters.

Wilson reminds us again and again that celebrity is not real life: "Life is everybody's personal untrained hammerhead shark," she writes, "full of thwacking emotional whiplash and spinal emergency, full of weighty grace and random threat." She's right, of course, that my unscripted drama runs every station, matinee, and feature of my life. Not one scene from my "real life" is worthy of an Oscar night montage because my scenes are way too messy, unphotogenic, and important.

Yet I still dream of Marilyn Monroe dreamers and gum-popping 80s extras, light-saturated orchestras and my hand shaking another hand in a high-school gym. These are touchstones in the emotional whiplash of my youth. They are the random, non-threatening flashes that give me an easy story to tell.

~

When I first met Walter White, I was in pretty bad shape. Incapacitated by depression and anxiety, I couldn't bring myself to concentrate on much of anything. But the moment I laid eyes on that desperate man trembling with a gun in his signature tighty whities, a bullet-riddled RV smoking in the desert behind him, I was transfixed.

I had always hated—actually, feared—violence and bloodshed. As a high school sophomore, I fainted during a film strip about making tourniquets. As a result, the drivers' ed department exempted me from viewing *Red Asphalt*, a body-strewn movie produced by my home state of California's Highway Patrol. But the next year I fainted in my history class as my teacher described his Vietnam injury. Well into adulthood, I continued to experience all manner of dizziness, nausea, and cold sweats when faced with suffering.

So why did I take instant interest, even comfort, in a man who lurched down a dirt road with unconscious, poisoned men rolling around the floor of an RV? Why me, the girl who did not attend one drinking party in high school or college and who has never lit, snorted, or injected a thing? With every reason to fill my mind with good things, why did I keep wanting to return to one of the most disturbing shows of all time?

Walt, and just about every other character on *Breaking Bad,* is a wild mess of unbridled human darkness. Watching them can make anyone feel better about their relative mere foibles. At least I'm not disappearing bodies in barrels of acid! But I don't believe mine is a case of moral superiority and its false reassurances.

Walking with Walt—and heartbreaking Jesse—in their desperation, a desperation more intense than what I face in my everyday worries and imbalances and fights with kids, comforted me because it made me feel more human. Life is far from stable for them, but they still get up every day with the power to make choices, as flawed and fraught as those choices are. I knew I could do the same.

As Walt says in the first episode, after Jesse questions him about his new direction in life, "I am awake."

Messed up, but awake.

Even as I began to find more chemical and emotional balance, I stuck with Walt. I couldn't leave him alone in the mess he was making of his life. When he stared at the broken plate in the trash can and realized what he had to do with his captor, I felt the weight of my own daily decisions churning in my gut. When he shaved his head for the first time, I felt parts of my old self falling away as I tried to make the best of who I was.

Walt always returns to past scenes from his life to "fix" things, much to the detriment of others. I had to make some amends myself.

I grew up just twenty miles from Hollywood but had never visited. The iconic sign and Walk of Fame were as mysterious as the pyramids to me. Though I was raised in a virtual wonderland of sights, a place people fly to from all over the world, my parents didn't like the stress of going much of anywhere. LA equaled the ends of the earth.

Visiting Hollywood was not a bucket list item as much as filling a gap, another California wound I had nurtured in my disdain and fascination for the state I had left. I've had to admit that parts of me remain—my childhood anxiety mixed with the quaking, sunny, polluted, adventurous, and stifling place as ugly and beautiful as my soul.

After buying cheap T-shirts (my son's has already shrunk to the size of a sports bra), squealing at chihuahuas in handbags, and snapping shadowy pictures of filthy sidewalk stars from Charlie Chaplin to Johnny Cash to Marilyn Monroe, I sought what I had really come for, the only star I was willing to touch.

In front of the Redbury Hotel at 1717 Vine Street, among smashed gum, cigarette butts, and the exhaust of an armored car, I lay by Bryan Cranston's name. My husband snapped a picture as the sizzling ground burned my elbows. Somehow, I'd made things right.

My hero is a middle-aged meth manufacturer, liar, thief and murderer, who convinces himself that his love for himself, his "growth, decay, and transformation"—the way he describes chemistry—is love for others. "Hero" is probably the wrong word. But I can watch Walt for hours, live in the deepening crevices of his face, ride his emotions and lies. This is what humans are capable of. I am not with Walt, but I can feel what he feels. And wake to life.

~

Every summer night, and weekends and holidays year-round,

Orange County comes under attack. At 9:25 p.m., the sky gets ripped apart by the happiest ballistics on earth, Disneyland's fireworks show. Even Rossmoor residents, living thirteen miles west of the park, can hear the distant rumble, the nightly reminder that when it comes to SoCal, the Mouse is boss. And yes, it means war.

Even when I was a small child, Disneyland was both my favorite place to visit and hate. In first grade, when one of my friends asked me what I did over winter break, I announced that I had seen the Long Beach Symphony Orchestra perform Beethoven's Fifth.

"Well, I had more fun. I went to Disneyland."

I rolled my eyes. "You don't know what music is," I said, and huffed off, wondering why I didn't have more friends.

But of course, on my seventh birthday that summer I asked to go to Disneyland. I wore my braids in scarlet-ribboned loops with a taffeta dress to match in recognition of this zenith of celebration: the Magic Kingdom.

Before 1982, guests purchased tickets at different prices for different levels of attractions, from sedate A's to exhilarating E's. None of us very adventurous, we bought ticket books lower on the D and E tickets and higher on the A to C's, focusing on Snow White more than Space Mountain.

I loved riding a shiny scowling lilac caterpillar on broad green leaves on Alice in Wonderland. I laughed every time the Jungle Cruise captain pointed to a pile of skulls and said they belonged to the last boatload of guests. I collected blown-glass animals from the crystal shop.

But still, I had trouble embracing Disneyland completely. I never wanted to hug Goofy or Cinderella or buy shirts plastered with Mickey's face. "What was your favorite part of the day?" my mom would ask as we pulled out of the massive parking lot, the Matterhorn still glowing behind us, my feet aching and my head throbbing from the crowds.

"Going home."

Everyone who grew up near Disneyland knew the stories. The cast member who got crushed during a performance of *America Sings*. The woman who died on the Matterhorn bobsled because of an unfastened seat belt (On purpose? We'll never know). The Skyway gondolas stalling for five hours, fire trucks rescuing people from 40 feet, after a rowdy guest disabled the emergency shut-off response.

There were the personal tragedies, too, like my nineteenth birthday trip, when the expensive gold bracelet my boyfriend had just given me flew off as we careened around a curve on Big Thunder Mountain Railroad. When we broke up a few months later, he was still paying it off.

Most of these stories evoke terror, not just because they are terrifying in themselves but because they destroy the illusion of Disney bliss in ways impossible to imagine. Blood. Heartache. Emergency vehicles. These are the kinds of things that happened on the 5 freeway.

After my nineteenth birthday trip, I took my mom as her Christmas gift. That was 1992, three years before the first *Toy Story* was released. Two years later, I moved.

Disney has not bewitched me. Jeremy and I are proud to have raised our daughters in a princess-free household, where women are more than twenty-inch waists waiting to be rescued. Mostly, we didn't want to train our children to blindly follow their dollars to trademarked merchandise. Finding underwear without characters on them was difficult. But we prevailed. When my daughter dressed as Cleopatra to a "princess-themed" costume party, her friends, dressed as Ariel and Belle and Cinderella, told her she did it wrong. She flipped her black, bejeweled wig and smirked, informing them she was the only real royalty at the ball.

On all our family trips back to California, we've focused on oceans, mountains, and relatives, not theme parks. The cost of tickets for a family of five would be enough to deplete most of our vacation budget, anyway. But starting around age 40, I wanted to go back. I couldn't shake the desire to climb aboard a Small World boat and sail across the aquamarine water. I wanted to hear animatronic children sing. I wanted to sit next to my mom. To be seven again.

I visited California one November, during which my mother and I, 81 and 45, ventured to Disneyland, just the two of us. We packed trail mix and carrot sticks into sensible Tupperware containers, ordered a Lyft, and rode into bustling Anaheim, which had exploded into more stores, restaurants, and hotels than I remembered.

We got our bags checked. We had our tickets scanned from my phone. And we walked into my childhood.

Main Street looked the same, its giant Christmas tree (it was November 15) towering in the same spot, then the magic shop and ice cream parlor and cinema and penny arcade and Sleeping Beauty's Castle, a giant, fake-snow-covered plaything, sparkling at the end of the road.

What was different a quarter of a century later was not so much the place, but the people, the simple felt Mickey ears replaced with hundreds of permutations of hats and headbands with sequins and leopard prints and mermaid scales and R2D2 flashing lights. People wore T-shirts announcing their intentions for their visit: Bride to Be. Honeymoon. First Time at Disney. Retired. Going to Disneyland was a rite of passage, not just a fun way to pass the time. With tickets starting at $98 per person, that was understandable. You prepared, commemorated, took selfies on the drawbridge, and shared to social media. Disneyland was the celebrity, and you were meeting and greeting with all you had.

What surprised me the most was how small the park had become in my middle-aged eyes. The entrances to Fantasyland, Tomorrowland, Frontierland, and Adventureland were all right there at the end of Main Street, just steps away from one another. What was once an endless, exhausting world was merely 160 acres jam-packed with vivid detail.

But we knew where to start. Immediately we turned left toward New Orleans Square and made our way to the Pirates of the Caribbean.

Before the attraction became a movie franchise, before pirates became all the rage, I loved this ride—the musty odor, the sound of water lapping against the boat, the terrifying drop under the skull and crossbones that signaled the beginning of the deep, dark journey at sea. We were boarded in the front of a boat that carried about a dozen other people, and immediately, without shame or irony, I cheered, clapped my hands, took selfies with my mom that wouldn't turn out in the dark.

After twenty-five years away, I recognized every detail like I had just seen it: the skeleton pirate sitting atop his gold-dripping mountain of loot, the dirty feet of the rum-drinking pirate lounging above us on the bridge, the cannon fire across the water (which made me laugh hysterically this time), and the scrappy dog holding the prison door key while the jailers try to cajole him through the bars.

After Pirates, we continued to move through the park with purpose, my mother stopping only occasionally to rest her legs on a bench, and soaked up all the images I had never realized helped define my youth: Peter Pan, and the tiny lights of London twinkling under our feet; the queen from Alice in Wonderland raising her fists and screaming, "Off with her head!" And, of course, It's a Small World, a ride I hadn't seen in a generation, decorated and soundtracked for Christmas, but still essentially the same. Forever-children hula danced in trembling skirts, popped out of tulips, and sang in the Andes with bright blue llamas, hundreds of faces more familiar than my mother's, for while hers was slowly aging and changing, theirs have been continually refreshed since 1955.

My mom and I ate on the patio of the same Frontierland Mexican restaurant we had visited twenty-five years ago, surrounded by fountains and painted tiles. We watched the Christmas parade from the window of the ice cream parlor. We examined every plant on every terrace, every lantern, every stone-carved raven and squirrel.

We didn't think we would make it the whole day, but we stayed almost a full twelve hours until the holiday fireworks show, watching the streams of light dripping above the castle from our tiny section of Main Street curb. At the grand finale, machines attached on the roofs of buildings blew out fake snow—spritzes of fluffy foam—which floated down on our heads. Neither of us was expecting this special touch, and when I turned to my mom, she was gazing up like a child seeing snow for the first time: mouth open, eyes big, cheeks shining.

Perfection. They did it again. The illusion of fantasy and wonder, and here I was falling for it, just one of 500 million visitors who have walked through that gate. I was giving in to Disneyland, but I had no energy to fight it. I didn't want to leave the park.

I have discovered that much of my relationship with California is giving in to it, giving in to the beautiful, dangerous geography with its earthquakes and mountains and waves, giving in to the sun beating through the windshield while sitting on the freeway, In-N-Out burger in hand. Giving in to the Hollywood sign that for a moment makes you feel famous just for looking at it.

Why would you ever leave California? I still hear every time I meet someone new. *Do you miss it?* I continue to chafe against those questions because they seem to dismiss the lives we've built here in the Midwest. I don't miss California enough to live there because it's simply been too long. When my plane descends into the flatlands of Milwaukee, my airport of choice, I exhale the sigh of home.

But you can never fully escape where you are from. You hold pieces of it inside like pirate's treasure, broken strings of pearls and tarnished coins buried under the wreckage of the past.

My mother moved from Wolf Point, Montana, to San Pedro, California, when she was one, then stayed in SoCal, which means her whole life has been without seasons, without snow, except for maybe a few trips to the San Bernardino mountains. When she was a baby, bundled up against the brutality of the Depression and the Montana sky, she undoubtedly had snowflakes on her lashes like she did on Main Street USA. She doesn't consciously remember Montana, but I like to believe she carries it with her, just as in spite of myself, I carry bursts of the legendary Santa Ana winds in my lungs, the searing hot whips of it, on those rare dry summer days in Illinois.

"Don't forget to take mom on the ride where you go through the whale's mouth," my sister had texted me the morning we left for Disneyland. She was referring to the Storybook Land Canal Boats, on which guests gather to be guided through several perfectly landscaped miniature lands from Disney films, including London Park from Peter Pan, the French countryside from Cinderella, and the dwarfs' cottage from Snow White. But before entering the magical land of thatched roofs and golden spires, you must pass through the mouth of Monstro, a large sculpted whale-cave modeled on the giant creature who swallows Pinocchio.

And this is where I will acquiesce that no one, no one can pass through that mouth with the huge white teeth hanging above them without experiencing a sense of wonder. I challenge anyone to ride on a gondola through the mouth of a whale into a land of flowers and miniature villages and not experience delight, even if just a tiny pulse of it—or the wish for it—in the body of an otherwise grim existence.

So my mother and I climbed on, just one gondola-load of people that the young man in a straw hat and khakis would guide today over a number of days, weeks, months. He would welcome us to Storybook Land in a sing-songy voice almost ironic in its lilt. "And here we go through the whaaaaaale," he said, his voice stepping down a half-tone as if we were small children. And for the moment we *were* children, preschoolers, even, looking up and smiling, totally dependent on our guide and the journey ahead, the sun filtering through a huge willow tree on shore and hitting Monstro's gums, my mom's gray hair catching a little bit of its old red fire.

BOOK CLUB DISCUSSION QUESTIONS

EARTHQUAKES

1. The author describes a host of items in this opening chapter. It's a powerful, seamless technique to create an impression on the reader and communicate subterranean meaning. Make a list of the items and reflect: how do they seem to both shape and mirror the author's inner life as a child and later as a teenager?

2. The author was left alone with "big forces" she couldn't control, beginning very early in life. Potentially, this contributed to the development of a life-long struggle with anxiety. Do you know anyone with anxiety? Is their journey similar? If you could help someone *not* develop anxiety—or try to cope with existing anxiety—where would you be inclined to start?

3. What is the function of control in a person's life? Do you believe it is negative or positive to want control?

4. At one point, the author visits The Mormon Rocks, as a way to "put them to rest." The first step is to "learn they had a name." Do you believe there is power in naming? What is the source of that power? Its result?

5. Why do you think some people are capable of seeking danger and others seem less inclined? What are the implications for society and for the individuals themselves?

FREEWAYS

1. Freeways are a staple of California life. What is a staple of the life you lead in your region? How are you affected by this, in ways either similar to or different from Californians' experience on their highways?

2. Joan Didion calls the California freeways a form of communion. What is a source of "communion" in your own region? If we wanted to create more "communion" in our country, how could we try to do that, so we could enjoy a sense of camaraderie even in the hard times?

3. When the author's father takes a "wrong" highway, a traumatic scene ensues. What was your own parents' response to things that went wrong? Has it affected your view of "mistakes," either positively or negatively?

4. "What *is* the real California, and can it ever be found?" asks the author about her home state. What *is* the real state *you* grew up in or live in now? And can it ever be found? What are the implications of that?

5. Have you ever tried to produce an epiphany from a symbolic gesture (the way the author tried to do by bringing home the ice plants for tea)? How successful were you, are you? What *do* you believe is the source of epiphanies? And is there a place for symbolic gesture in bringing illumination to a life?

6. Throughout the book, the author sometimes feels like she

does not understand her mother's penchant for art, curation, and collection. Yet they do hold these qualities in common at some level. How so?

BURBS

1. Going back to her childhood home, the author isn't sure what she is accomplishing once she's there. What do you believe she did or didn't accomplish? Have you ever gone back to your own childhood home? What did the experience accomplish or not accomplish for you?

2. The suburbs are discussed as a kind of dream or fantasyland—especially the Rossmoor development. What are the up and down sides to dreams and fantasies?

3. The author has a tenuous relationship with "the touchable things of the world." What do you believe contributed to that? (Go ahead, conjecture.) What is your own relationship to objects? How do they either enrich or complicate your life—or both?

4. One afternoon on her way to the beach, the author's father tries to join her in a bike ride that ends a bit tragically (for him). Before he even fell down, what was the tragedy unfolding in that moment? Should he not have tried to bond with his daughter?

5. How does the tortoise story contribute to our understanding of the growing relationship between the author and her

mom, after years of tentativeness between mother and daughter?

THE BEACH BOYS

1. Living in California was not an easy arena in which a girl could learn to love her body and explore a healthy way to move through the world of relationship. Can you relate, even if you grew up elsewhere? What makes it easy and hard to love our bodies?

2. Explore the question of power in relationships, sexual or otherwise. What are the dangers? Is there any positive to it?

3. What are the boundaries of self in relation to geography, art, commerce? Is there any such thing as a strictly independent self? How does this interact with the American dream?

4. The author's father is a hard man to relate to, at least for her. What are some of the first indications that she has begun to understand this person who feels so outside of her—even at times in violation of her? What might this eventually achieve in her life? And what, if you face a similar situation, might such understanding achieve in yours?

5. Arguably, the author forgave her father for his anxieties and angers (less so, his indiscretions). However, she did not forget them. Describe the edges of forgiveness for yourself. Where do they begin and end for you? How do you deal with a person who never really changes but whom you can't quite erase

from your life and memories—and possibly don't want to either?

6. The question was raised: "What did it mean to be a daughter?" Let's think on that. What *does* it mean to be a daughter? A son? And are these different in relation to a father, a mother? How did the author's father exhibit a certain philosophy in these regards?

STARS

1. Define "celebrity." Is there any positive function for celebrities in society and your personal life? Conversely, are there any truly negative impacts?

2. Have you ever been to Hollywood? What was the experience like? Did you get a photograph with an actual or sidewalk star? How did/does that make you feel? Do you tell the story—why or why not?

3. How do you feel about being on camera, or screen? Do you seek or avoid it? Regardless of whether you personally enjoy being on camera or screen, how do you feel about others who are? Is there some kind of transcendence that enters the picture? Power? Immortality?

3. Have you ever been empowered by a film, story, or poem? In what way were they "real" to you or not?

4. What makes Disney so different from an ordinary amuse-

ment park? What gives it such power to serve as a "rite of passage"?

5. Going to Disneyland is the ultimate fantasy, and, in the end, the author returns there with her mom. What is the positive side of fantasy and wonder? Looking back at the whole memoir, where do you see evidence that fantasy, wonder, and imagination may be the very things that got the author through childhood and then on a journey to deeper healing as an adult?

6. "You can never fully escape where you are from," notes the author. A few paragraphs later, she willingly takes a plunge into the fanciful jaws of a storybook whale on a Disney ride. How does this ride-journey relate to the statement about escape—an action which had been her errand since she was a child first opening that World Atlas?

7. Did the author, in your opinion, make peace with anything in her life? What indicates to you that she did or didn't? How have you personally made peace with certain things in your own life?

NOTES

Earthquakes

p. 7: *Hammond Ambassador World Atlas.* Maplewood, New Jersey, Hammond Incorporated, 1980.

p. 13: CBS Los Angeles. "Southern California Air Pollution Kills Thousands Annually, Study Says." *Cbslocal.Com*, CBS Los Angeles, 10 Aug. 2016, losangeles.cbslocal.com/2016/08/10/southern-california-air-pollution-leads-to-thousands-of-avoidable-deaths-annually-study-says/. Accessed 22 Sept. 2016.

p. 15: Rice, Doyle. "'It's Only a Question of Time': California Is Overdue for a Massive Earthquake." *USA TODAY*, USA TODAY, 18 Apr. 2018, www.usatoday.com/story/news/nation/2018/04/18/california-earthquakes-when-big-one-hit/527732002/. Accessed 12 Apr. 2017.

p. 16: Dvorak, John. *Earthquake Storms: An Unauthorized Biography of the San Andreas Fault.* S.L., Pegasus Books, 2014.

p. 20: "Mormon Rocks Interpretive Trail." USDA Forest Service. https://www.fs.usda.gov/Internet/FSE_DOCUMENTS/stelprdb5391972.pdf. Accessed 30 March 2017.

Freeways

p. 26: Masters, Nathan. "Why Southern Californians Love Saying 'the' Before Freeway Numbers." *KCET*, 10 Nov. 2015, www.kcet.org/shows/lost-la/the-5-the-101-the-405-why-southern-californians-love-saying-the-before-freeway-numbers. Accessed 23 Sept. 2016.

p. 27: Starr, Kevin. *Golden Dreams: California in an Age of Abundance: 1950-1963*. New York, Oxford University Press, 2011.

p. 28: Didion, Joan. *The White Album*. London 4Th Estate, 2017.

p. 28: Sanchez, Ana. "Comment on Facebook Post." 11 Sept. 2016.

p. 31 Brodsky, David. *L.A. Freeway, an Appreciative Essay*. Berkeley, University Of California Press, 1983.

p. 35: Journey. "Any Way You Want It." *Departure*, Columbia, 1980.

p. 37: J'aime Rubio, author. "The Rea Family & Katella Ranch." *Blogspot.Com*, 23 Jan. 2020, anaheimhistory.blogspot.com/2014/07/the-rea-family-katella-ranch.html. Accessed 20 Jul. 2017.

p. 37: Spitzer, Gabriel. "Ice Plant Getting Cold Reception From Naturalists." *Los Angeles Times*, Los Angeles Times, 4 May 2002, www.latimes.com/archives/la-xpm-2002-may-04-me-outthere4-story.html. Accessed 29 Jul. 2017.

p. 40: Eidt, John. "Los Angeles River Revitalization: A City Rediscovers Its Flow | *WilderUtopia.Com*." WilderUtopia.Com, 9 Apr. 2013, www.wilderutopia.com/sustainability/land/los-angeles-river-revitalization-city-rediscovers-flow/. Accessed 22 Sept. 2016.

p. 40: Hinton, Tilly. "Thesis Snippets: Paint, Cats, and the L.A. River." *Good Is Better*, 4 Jan. 2017, http://goodisbetter.net/thesis-snippets-paint-cats-and-the-l-a-river. Accessed 20 Jan. 2020.

p. 42: Limon, Leo. "Welcome to the Official Website for Leo

	Limon." *Leolimon.Com*, 2017, leolimon.com/home.html. Accessed 19 Sept. 2016.
p. 44:	Glendale Narrows — Earth Iron. "Earth Iron." *Earth Iron*, 2014, earthiron.net/glendale-narrows-2. Accessed 28 Sept. 2016.

Burbs

p. 48:	Rossmoor. "History." *Ourrossmoor.Com*, 2015, ourrossmoor.com/history/. Accessed 28 May. 2017.
p. 48:	Waldie, D J. *Holy Land a Suburban Memoir*. W.W. Norton, 2005.
p. 55:	Strawther, Larry. *A Brief History of Los Alamitos & Rossmoor*. The History Press, 2012.
p. 56:	*The Summer Hours*. Directed by Olivier Assayas, MK2 Productions, 2008.
p. 58:	Remnet, Art. "RHA Website Contact Request." 18 Sept. 2017.
p. 60:	"An Air-Taxi Helicopter Lost Its Tail Rotor and Crashed..." *UPI,* UPI, 7 Nov. 1983, www.upi.com/Archives/1983/11/07/An-air-taxi-helicopter-lost-its-tail-rotor-and-crashed/3167437029200/. Accessed 1 Aug. 2016.

Beach Boys

p. 68:	The Dream Academy. "Life in a Northern Town." *The Dream Academy,* Warner Bros., 1984.
p. 77:	The Beach Boys. "California Girls." *Summer Days (And Summer Nights!!)*, Capitol, 1965.

p. 78: The Beach Boys. *Pet Sounds*, Capitol, 1966.

p. 78: *Love & Mercy*. Directed by Bill Pohlad, Lionsgate/Roadside Attractions, 2014.

p. 79: Wilson, Brian. *I Am Brian Wilson*. Hodder & Stoughton, 2017.

p. 79: Beard, David. "Discover the Story behind The Beach Boys' 'SMiLE.'" *Goldmine Magazine*, 5 Jan. 2012, www.goldminemag.com/articles/discover-the-story-behind-the-beach-boys-smile. Accessed 8 Oct. 2017.

p. 80: Finnegan, William. *Barbarian Days: A Surfing Life*. London, Corsair, 2016.

p. 82: "The Beach Boys - Sloop John B Promo Film (Official Video)." *YouTube*, 3 Mar. 2009, www.youtube.com/watch?v=nSAoEf1Ib58. Accessed 6 Jan. 2017.

p. 83: Sandburg, Carl. *The American Songbag* by Carl Sandburg. Harcourt, 1927.

p. 83: The Kingston Trio. "The Kingston Trio," Capitol, 1958.
p. 84: Harry Belafonte. "Mark Twain and Other Folk Favorites," RCA Victor, 1954.

p. 84: *Carousel*. Directed by Henry King, 20th Century Fox, 1956.

Stars

p. 90: *Calendar Girl*. Directed by John Whitesell, Columbia Pictures, 1993.

p. 90: *Like Father, Like Son*. Directed by Rod Daniel, TriStar Pictures,

1987.

p. 91: *L.A. County Holiday Celebration.* KCET, 1986.

p. 92: *First Blood.* Directed by Ted Kotcheff, Orion Pictures, 1982.

p. 93: *Teacher of the Year.* Focus on the Family, 1990.

p. 96: Wilson, Cintra. *A Massive Swelling: Celebrity Re-Examined as a Grotesque, Crippling Disease, and Other Cultural Revolutions.* Viking, 2000.

p. 97: "Pilot." *Breaking Bad*, season 1, episode 1, AMC, 20 Jan. 2008.

p. 97: *Red Asphalt.* California Highway Patrol, 1964.

REFERENCES

This book contains references to the following companies, brands, and sources: Waldenbooks; *Three's Company*, NRW Productions and T.T.C Productions, Inc., 1977-1984; Disneyland; *Ramona the Brave*, by Beverly Cleary, William Morrow, 1975; *Wheel of Fortune*, Merv Griffin Productions/Enterprises (1975-1994); Honda Accord; Gatorade is a registered trademark of PepsiCo; Grateful Dead; Steer and Stein; *Phantom of the Opera,* Andrew Lloyd Webber, 1986; Superman ride, Six Flags Great America; *Saturday Night Live*, Broadway Video; Jack in the Box; In-N-Out Burger; Plymouth Fury is a registered trademark of Chrysler Corporation; Toyota Corolla; Knott's Berry Farm, Cedar Fair Entertainment Company; Lucky Market, American Stores; M&Ms is a registered trademark of Mars, Inc.; Ford Bronco, Ford Motor Company; U-Haul, AMERCO; Del Taco, Jack in the Box; Coppertone is a registered trademark of Beiersdorf; *Love Boat,* Aaron Spelling Productions; Self Help Graphics; Aquafina is a registered trademark of PepsiCo; Google Maps, Chemex is a registered trademark of Chemex Corporation; Duran Duran; Hello Kitty is a registered trademark of Sanrio; Garfield is a registered trademark of Viacom; Google Earth; McDonnell Douglas (Boeing); Mercedes; Scholastic Corporation; Rene Gruau; *The Cat in the Hat,* by Dr. Seuss, Random House/Houghton Mifflin, 1957; *Munyurangabo*, Almond Tree Films, 2007; *Downton Abbey,* ITV; "Life In a Northern Town," *The Dream Academy,* The Dream Academy, Warner Bros., 1985; Walkman is a registered trademark of Sony; *Playboy,* Playboy Enterprises; Ruby's Diner; Humane Society of the United States; Cold Stone Creamery, Kahala Brands; UGG, Deckers Brands; The Beatles; Erasure; Siouxsie and the Banshees; *Maranatha Praise,* Volume 6, Maranantha, 1989; Jell-O is a registered trademark of Kraft Foods Group; *Pet Sounds,* The Beach Boys, Capitol Records, 1966 (including the songs, "Dance, Dance, Dance," "Little Deuce Coupe," "In My Room," "God Only Knows," "Sloop John B"); *The SMiLE Sessions,* The Beach Boys, Universal, 2011; Spotify; Jack in the Box; *The Kingston Trio,* The Kingston Trio, Capitol Records, 1958 (including the songs, "Scotch and Soda," "Saro Jane," "Little Maggie," "Three Jolly Coachmen, " and "Sloop John B"; *South Pacific,* Richard Rodgers and Oscar Hammerstein II, 1949; "Soliloquy," *Carousel,* Richard Rodgers and Oscar Hammerstein II, 1945; Bugs Bunny is a registered trademark of Warner Bros. Entertainment; *Some Like it Hot,* United Artists, 1959; "Rudolph the Red-Nosed Reindeer," John David Marks, St. Nicolas Music Publishing Company, 1949; "Sleigh Bells," Leroy Anderson. Mills Music, 1948; Focus on the Family; *Molder of Dreams,* Focus on the Family, 1989; YouTube; ebay; Lyft; Disneyland is a registered trademark of the Walt Disney Company, as are the following park features, rides, and characters: Snow White, E-ticket, Space Mountain, Alice in Wonderland, Jungle Cruise, Matterhorn, Skyway, Big Thunder Mountain Railroad, It's a Small World, Fantasyland, Tomorrowland, Frontierland, Adventureland, Main Street, Sleeping Beauty's Castle, New Orleans Square, Pirates of the Caribbean, Peter Pan, Storybook Land Canal Boats, Goofy, Cinderella, Ariel, Belle, and "America Sings"; *Cinderella,* Walt Disney Productions, 1950; *Snow White*, Walt Disney Productions, 1937; *Peter Pan*, Walt Disney Productions, 1953; *Toy Story*, Walt Disney Pictures, 1995; R2D2 is a registered trademark of Lucasfilm Entertainment Company Ltd.

Also from T. S. Poetry Press

The Yellow Wall-Paper: A Graphic Novel —
full text by Charlotte Perkins Gilman, 1892
Illustrations by Sara Barkat, 2020

Made in United States
North Haven, CT
17 October 2022

25562260R00074